From Cape Wrath To Finisterre

by
Björn Larsson

Translated from the Swedish by
Tom Geddes

Armchair Traveller
at the bookHaus

First published in Swedish by Norstedts Förlag, Stockholm, 2000,
under the title *Från Vredens Kap till Jordens Ände*

Copyright © Björn Larsson 2000
Copyright © 2003 by marebuchverlag, Hamburg/Germany
All rights reserved

English translation copyright © Tom Geddes 2005

First published in English in 2005 by Haus Publishing Limited

This paperback edition published in 2012 by
The Armchair Traveller *at the bookHaus*
70 Cadogan Place
London SW1X 9AH
www.thearmchairtraveller.com

A CIP catalogue record for this book is available from the British Library

ISBN: 978-1-907973-18-5
ebook ISBN: 978-1-907973-30-7

Typeset in Garamond by MacGuru Ltd
info@macguru.org.uk
Printed and bound in the UK by CPI Group (UK) Ltd, Croydon, CR0 4YY

Contents

Translator's Note

Most of the quotations from Harry Martinson's *Cape Farewell (Kap Farväl!*, 1933) are based on the translation by Naomi Walford, London: The Cresset Press, 1934. Martinson's *Aimless Travels (Resor utan mål*, 1932) has not been published in English translation.

Our ideal should not be the calm,
which can turn the very ocean to a stagnant pool,
nor the hurricane, but the mighty trade-wind,
fresh, life-giving and unfailing.

Harry Martinson: *Cape Farewell*
(Translated by Naomi Walford)

On Rootlessness, Restlessness and Liberty

There is a splendid English expression, poetic licence. In Swedish we talk a little more prosaically of 'poetic freedom': that is, in the realm of words, the right of the poet, novelist or dramatist to take liberties with reality and language – most often, paradoxically enough, in order to convey the truth of something.

In choosing my title for this book, *From Cape Wrath to Finisterre*, I have taken advantage of this authorial liberty. I have never seen Cape Wrath, other than in a picture. I could also mention that Cape Wrath does not mean, as one might assume, anger: wrath is from the Old Norse *hvaif*, meaning 'turning point'. It was actually named by the Vikings on their constant voyages between the Orkneys and the Outer Hebrides, both of which were under Norse rule for several centuries.

On the other hand, *Cabo Finisterre*, the furthest point of Spain or Galicia jutting out into the Atlantic, is a place I have seen and sailed past at close quarters, in a northerly gale that blew up in minutes. And Finisterre really does mean the End of the Earth or World's End. Though Cape Finisterre is not, as was once thought, the westernmost point of Europe. That honour goes to Ireland – if we ignore a few smaller islands such as Iceland, the Canaries and Madeira.

I could not resist the poetic resonance I thought a title like *Cape Wrath to Finisterre* would convey. But I am aware that I cannot attempt to hide the truth from my readers; this is not a novel, after all.

What is it, then?

A travel book? In a way. Musings on life seen from the cockpit and deck of a yacht? Certainly. The journal of a voyage? That too, but not in logbook form. A homage to Celtic lands and waters? That is my intention. A source of inspiration for those who dream of living a different kind of life? I hope so. But above all I hoped that *From Cape Wrath to Finisterre* would inspire more people to read Harry Martinson's *Resor utan mål* (Aimless Travels, 1932) and *Cape Farewell* (1933, English translation London 1934), which I nominate without the slightest hesitation as two of the foremost travel accounts in literature, way ahead of today's over-hyped travel writers like Chatwin or Theroux.

If Harry Martinson had written in a world language such as English, I venture to assert that he would have provided both a model and an unattainable ideal for present-day exponents of the genre. Unfortunately Martinson is linguistically so original and creative that he is virtually untranslatable. Philippe Bouquet, who must be one of the most skilful translators of Swedish literature into other languages, made an attempt into French but gave up (or at least postponed his endeavours), because he did not want to give a diluted and insipid version of Martinson's inimitable Swedish.

All the more reason for us who have the advantage of knowing Swedish to read Martinson over and over again. For his works are not just linguistic virtuosity, they also offer a vision of life and reality which is more pertinent now than ever. At its heart is a homage to mankind as nomad and traveller. '*Perhaps,*' he writes in *Aimless Travels*, '*wanderlust might prove to be mankind's deepest urge, once hunger and love were satisfied.*'

Many critics have pointed out that Martinson, unlike many writers, viewed reality and the world in a broad perspective, as well as focussing more sharply on its details than most others. Both aspects are illustrated in these two sentences: '*I saw wooden benches there as elsewhere in the world, and on them sat men waiting for help. I sat there for a week but no help came.*'

While I was writing *From Cape Wrath to Finisterre,* for a long time I had no thought of Harry Martinson. It was only in the final phase, when I was re-reading for about the tenth time the two books mentioned above, that it occurred to me that Martinson had already expressed most of what I was saying, but better and more stylishly. That was why I decided to add his words as commentaries on my own adventures, thoughts and experiences.

I am aware of the risks inherent in such a procedure: the difference in poetry and depth of thought between my own and Martinson's writing is all too obvious. But there is no reason to prevaricate: neither I nor any number of other travel writers of greater or lesser calibre can measure up to him.

It would gratify me nevertheless if my experiences and cockpit philosophising might have something to offer both sailors and landlubbers. I have not sailed round the world like Martinson, but I have sailed. I may not have been a true vagabond like Martinson, but I feel I have not always restricted my life to the main channels, so to speak, and that for this reason alone it just might be of interest to others.

By most normal criteria I could be regarded as a rootless and restless soul, one of those people whose *deepest urge is wanderlust*. Until I reached the age of forty I had never lived more than a few years at the same address, if I exclude the postbox where I was registered for tax purposes for four years. I managed to avoid permanent employment until I was forty. Life, I thought, and still think, should be interrupted at most by commas, semicolons or dashes. There will come a full-stop eventually anyway.

For a long time I had almost no possessions, no car, no TV, no telephone, no furniture, just a boat with the usual equipment and a dozen shelves of books lodged with friends. Of the previous twenty years I had spent the lion's share abroad: four years in France, fifteen in Denmark, one in Ireland and two afloat in the north Atlantic. For six years I lived all year round on board my sailing yacht *Rustica*, and can honestly say that I have never been happier. Both *Rustica* and I were in our element without a permanent base.

Most recently we sailed in Celtic waters, around what is called the 'Celtic fringe': Scotland, Ireland, Wales, Brittany and Galicia. Perhaps I was looking for a homeland, perhaps not, or at any rate a place where it would be worth trying to live for a while as well as one can for as long as it lasts. My assumption was the simplest imaginable: that we only have one life and that there is no advantage in being immortal on the other side of the grave.

So I admit to rootlessness, in the highest degree, but as a resource, as an opportunity to be able to choose for oneself to put down roots where the soil is most fertile; no more, in fact, than what mankind has been doing since time immemorial.

But perhaps I am playing with the truth again. For in fact my only native country is travelling, even if it is only a commuter trip from Gilleleje, in Denmark, where I live at the moment, to Lund, in Sweden, where I work, or a longish voyage into foreign waters. It is only when I am travelling that I feel really content. At least it is only then, on a train or even lying back in an aircraft seat, but above all on *Rustica*, that I live in the present. In general I want too much. There are a hundred lives I would like to live, a thousand books to write, even more to read, new people to meet and love or befriend, all sorts of things, stones to find and polish, starry skies to observe, scholarly theories to research, new waters to sail. And so on and so forth. I would like many lives, but have to accept the fact that I only have one.

Nor is it easy, as Wittgenstein put it, to find the solution to life's problems by living in such a way as to make those problems vanish, or more specifically to be able to sail around for a while completely free in order to find the places where it is worth lingering.

But it is possible.

It is possible to make some time for it. It is possible to live a life which is a little different from the one prescribed. When I was twenty I set off by train to Paris on a single ticket with two suitcases and the equivalent of £2,000 savings in my pocket. My intention was to live in Paris until the money ran out. Friends asked me if it wasn't 'risky' or thought I displayed 'courage'. But what constitutes courage? As long as I had enough money for my return ticket I had no need for courage. I stayed a year, renting a maid's room, a *chambre de bonne* in the attic, and lived a life much as

I could have wished, albeit poverty-stricken. But there was no need for courage. Just a little initiative.

Yes, I admit to rootlessness and impermanence. But restlessness, on the other hand, is a scourge. It and its modern variant, stress, *the futility of running round in circles*, are to be avoided at all costs.

~

In essence, then, the subject of this book is one attempt among many to live in a way that makes life's problems vanish. It is based on a yacht called *Rustica* and a love of Celtic waters, landscapes and peoples. It is far from certain, of course, that this way of life would suit everybody. But if it instils in some the desire to experiment with alternatives, I shall be happy. If it can inspire some to take liberties with life, I shall be happy. If it can also inspire some to discover Harry Martinson, I shall be happy.

Completely happy.

'*As you've found out,*' Martinson says to a little milliner-girl he rescued from a prison in Santiago, '*the world's a damned difficult place. You have to look out for yourself among the scheming foxes and vegetating worms that overpopulate it.*'

(*Cape Farewell*)

On travelling

It was early autumn in Kinsale on the south coast of Ireland. *Rustica* and I had taken up winter quarters after three months' sailing in Celtic waters, from Lochskipport on South Uist in the north to Baltimore in Ireland in the south. It had been an unforgettable time, lending itself to effortless recall with perfect clarity of every single day experienced.

Helle, my companion in life and on board, was in Denmark for a few months working to replenish the boat's coffers. This arrangement aroused not just astonishment but also envious admiration among the male sailors I met during my lone voyage from Dublin to Kinsale. There were many who found it hard to believe that anyone could arrange life afloat so conveniently. One of them even called down to his own wife in the galley, 'Did you hear that? He's sent his wife home to earn money so that he can sail!'

While waiting for Helle to return I received a visit from my good friend Torben. He is no sailor, but he has most of the other qualities that make a friendship like his indispensable. And he is the most well-read person I know.

Among the writers he holds in the highest esteem, Samuel Beckett has pride of place. Torben has Beckett's works at his fingertips and can quote long passages from memory with ease. He had noticed for instance that somewhere in the middle of the novel *Molloy* one of the characters is described as sitting down on the bench exactly like Walter.

'But the fact is,' Torben explained, 'that Walter occurs nowhere else in the novel except as a gap on that bench.'

Anyone can see that it takes a very thorough knowledge of an author's work to be able to identify its lacunae.

Torben was full of expectations prior to his visit to Ireland. He was hoping to discover some hidden depths in Beckett's writing. Because even though Beckett had gone into exile in disappointment at his then bigoted and narrow-minded homeland, Torben was convinced that Ireland had left a profound imprint on him; so profound that a foreigner would not be able to discern it immediately by simply reading the texts.

Torben and I took long walks in the higher countryside around Kinsale. We would often head for a small village in which we were sure of finding a pub where we could drink a pint of fairly insipid ale and eat a sandwich. One day we were on our way to the village of Ballinspittle to see the famous Madonna that was rumoured to move when breath – or rather the spirit – moved her. (It's not beyond the bounds of possibility of course that the first person to see her rock back and forth was an Irishman staggering home from the pub!) A few years previously the fidgety Madonna had inspired tens of thousands of Irish folk to make a pilgrimage to this insignificant village nestling in its valley. Loudspeakers still stood on each side of the three-foot-high statue.

Not far from Kinsale, on the south side of the River Bandon and to the west, the whole landscape appears to rise. After a lengthy climb you reach a plateau and have the deep blue Atlantic on one side and Ireland's fresh green pastures as far the eye can see to the north.

Torben and I were walking along narrow tracks between meadows and ruminating cows, where you hardly met a soul. The only thing to exercise your mind was where to put your feet, because there were large cowpats everywhere.

Suddenly Torben came to a halt in mid-stride.

'Now I understand!' he exclaimed.

'What?'

'Why there's so much cow dung in Beckett's books!'

He had often wondered why Beckett seemed so obsessed by the consistency and smell of cow dung. Here was the explanation. Beckett must have walked on cattle tracks like these. He had inhaled these same aromas. He, like us, had been suspended between heaven and earth, with incomparable views and crystal-clear air, yet found it permeated by the stench of newly-dropped cow dung.

Torben and I discussed this and it struck me that we would never have made the discovery had we not been on foot. It is not even certain that the impression would have had time to sink in if we had been on bicycles. In a car, of course, it would have been out of the question. If travelling is about experiencing, as distinct from being transported from one place to another, then the value of the journey is in inverse proportion to the speed with which it is undertaken.

~

One evening in Tréguier, the old episcopal city built entirely of Brittany granite in the shadow of its immense cathedral, Helle and I sat over a bottle of excellent wine in *Rustica*'s cabin. We were sharing memories of our trip from Copenhagen via Scotland to Ireland, Cornwall and now Brittany, where we were once again about to spend the winter in harbour. Without even opening the logbook we could recount every single day of sailing, the lustre and hue of the sea, the strength of the wind, our degrees of tiredness on the morning watch, the fishing boat that passed in the middle of the North Sea with a pipe-smoking fisherman sitting in the lee of the wheelhouse as if he were basking in the sun on a park bench, the silence on the isle of Canna, the boiling current as we skirted Corryvreckan, our anxiety when we lay at anchor beneath the high mountains of Rhum and started to roll from side to side at dead of night in a growing swell from an unexpected direction, the giant seal sporting in Ardglass harbour, the short steep seas off Cap Fréhel where we met *Le Renard*, St-Malo's newly built replica of Surcouf's famous corsair ship – we could remember everything with particular clarity and precision.

A few days later I happened to be looking at an old map of Brittany that I had acquired when I had cycled along the north coast, and on which

I had marked in my route. Imagine my surprise when I discovered that I had cycled through Tréguier then. But my memory was a complete blank, despite the fact that Tréguier with its huge cathedral is definitely not a town like any other. I tried to recall the daily stages of my cycle trip, but could remember only fragments, a beach, a hotel, a smile, a kiss, making love on a rock, and an emaciated dog that someone had abandoned to its fate on a camp site. Heartrending. The dog had never dared leave the camp site because it was there it had last seen its owner.

On the other hand I remember perfectly well, sharply etched on my mind, the walk I did some years earlier from Dieppe to Fécamp along the chalk cliffs of the Normandy coast.

Travelling, Torben and I decided, meant experiencing. But there is a speed for experience, our own speed, not that of our means of conveyance. Sailing is a slow method of travel, as long as you're not competing in extremely shallow-draughted miracles of speed, designed and built for sport, which at sea means yachtracing. The *Rustica* has at best an average speed of five knots, or five and a half miles an hour, which is not much more than a fast walk. Seen in that light it is hardly surprising that it usually takes a couple of years to sail round the world. In principle it is the same as walking the whole way. It took us three days, two nights and five hours to sail across the North Sea, from Thyborøn in Jutland to Fraserburgh on the eastern tip of Scotland. To walk the same distance, 380 miles, roughly from Malmö to Stockholm or London to Edinburgh, might have taken another twenty-four hours on top of that, assuming you could walk non-stop. Cycling over the North Sea would have been considerably faster. An ordinary touring cyclist could have done it in two days and a night, a racing cyclist in fifteen hours.

I feel sure that the majority of those who sail would agree with me that sailing has a remarkable capacity for creating strong and lasting experiences and impressions. To sail is to remember. Because you have the time to commit to memory what you pass on the way.

I flew home from Ireland in two hours. I remember nothing of this so-called journey. Flying is the transportation of cargo, even though we are human. The only thing we (I) require is for it to be over as soon as possible. It is no help to be served a glass of free champagne.

No generalisations should be pursued *ad absurdum*, of course. There are so many opinions in this world on everything, even travelling. Robert Louis Stevenson wrote, 'I travel not to go anywhere, but to go. I travel for travel's sake.' Compare this with Samuel Beckett's rather different view in another context, that we don't travel simply for the pleasure of travelling, which he would regard as idiocy.

And we can learn from Harry Martinson that it is not enough to transport oneself at the right speed:

> Six times more swiftly than the cruising packets in the days of sail do our steamers voyage round the world. Constant change, motion and distances make up our life's adventure. Awake and eager we see a vast amount, but if we are sluggish and indifferent one horizon is very like another.

> (*Cape Farewell*)

So you have to want to keep your eyes open too.

Wide open.

On people

I'm the sort of person who finds others fascinating. Not that I imagine for a moment that people are inherently good. Nor evil, for that matter. Experience suggests that the diversity of human behaviour and character is limitless. Any degree of good or bad is feasible. To assert otherwise must be at best wishful thinking; at worst, stupidity.

Within the bounds of moderation and morality, that is precisely what is so fascinating, the richness of variation and nuance, the multiplicity of style and manner. What interests me most is finding out what others think about life, how they strive, if they strive at all, to live a life that is as satisfying as it could possibly be. What does happiness consist of for them? What is the extent of their dreams?

~

We met a lot of people during our ten thousand nautical miles of sailing. Some we still keep up with and number among our friends. Peter and Jette whom I met in Kinsale and who now live all year round with their two children on a wooden barge in Copenhagen that they built themselves and from which they row the children to school by dinghy. Jørn and Marianne, who are equivocal about life afloat and life ashore, which has led them to sell and buy boats the way others change their cars.

The majority have been just fleeting but nevertheless meaningful acquaintances for a few days. Where are they now? How has their life ashore panned out? Or are they still sailing the high seas?

There was Junior in the steel-hulled boat he had welded together with his own hands, who used to worry about everything and could hardly sail, yet got to Gibraltar single-handed. Where is he now? And Erling and Gry whom I met in Kinsale in their Colin Archer *Gryling*, as broad and steady as a toad. They had spent five years sailing round the world working for their food and boat maintenance as they went. But money had always been in short supply on board, to the extent that they had invented a new dictum, 'No money, no worry!' They sent me a postcard to say they were back safe and sound in their home port in northern Norway. But after that?

There was the jovial, tanned and one-toothed skipper of the *Eliza* who had sailed the Atlantic several times, and was every time 'bored to tears'. Now he was taking it easy in the Scottish islands. He said he had had enough of 'pushing around'. Is he still sailing the Hebrides? And what about Joe, the Scot who towed us into Falmouth after engine failure? Joe had earned his living in an atomic submarine that was under water for six months at a stretch. He it was who said that the world smelt rotten, that a dreadful stench filled the nostrils when the hatches of the submarine were opened as it surfaced for the first time in six months. We know that Joe went to the Mediterranean, because Helle ran into him a year later on Majorca, where she had gone to sail with her sister. But then the trail went cold. Or Joyce and Bill whom we met in Camariñas in Galicia and who treated us to champagne when they learnt that Helle was pregnant. This was the couple who had struck a bargain: first they would drive around for five years in a camper van for her sake and then sail for five years for his sake. The problem was that Joyce discovered she was frightened to death and panic-stricken as soon as she started sailing. Yet they had sailed as far as Galicia and had to get back home, five hundred nautical miles across the Bay of Biscay and the Irish Sea. How did their crossing go? What effect did her fear of sailing and his love of adventure have on their life thereafter? There was Yann on the yacht *Tadjoura* whom we met on the Ile de Groix in southern Brittany. He was a captain in the merchant navy. But as if he could not get enough of the sea, he spent all his free time sailing around Brittany, often on the hunt for local culinary specialities from whatever area he had made his own for a few days or weeks. He always sailed alone and only took guests or friends on board when he was in harbour. We have seldom seen anyone who could manoeuvre a sailing boat as calmly and surely as he could. He was a real professional, making the rest of us look like amateurs. Where is he and his First now? Or is he standing on the bridge of a ship on some far distant ocean?

There was an elderly couple in a 24-foot wooden boat who invited us in for a drink in Tobermory. Both over seventy, they lived in a cheap two-roomed apartment in Glasgow during the winter and spent the rest of the year sailing in a leisurely fashion around the Hebrides. That was their life and they intended to continue it until they could no longer cope. She excused herself when we came in for not standing up to greet us. She had hurt her back hauling in the anchor and chain a few days before, at 72 years of age. Are they still sailing? Are they still alive?

Among others we met were Dermott, Diana and their son, who was just called 'the little one', in Baltimore in south-west Ireland. The family got by with a dozen cows, a few casual jobs in the winter and running a sailing school in summer. They had a modest inherited house near the harbour with a view of the sea, they picked berries and went fishing, they seldom drank wine, and ate as cheaply and well as they could. Dermott said they managed fine on £7,000 a year, and they had all the time in the world for living and enough over for gradually building a 40-foot steel-hulled yacht. Dermott and Diana led a quiet and alternative lifestyle. They were happy, enjoyed life to the full and would not change with anyone for anything. Where are they now? Their plan was to cruise around Galicia and Portugal in winter, and spend the summer running their sailing school. I hope they succeeded. Dermott could certainly sail. The very day a terrible storm sank boats and crews off Fastnet he was out sailing for pleasure.

In the steeply-enclosed fishing port of Cudillero we met Rolf, a Norwegian who could not speak a word of Norwegian, but was an expert on cognac and sailed his little Norwegian-ensigned boat from Bordeaux to the north coast of Spain every year. He was one of seven sons of a Norwegian emigrant father who had become a brandy-merchant in France. His father had wanted at least one of his sons to have Norwegian nationality and Rolf had volunteered, despite being born and brought up in France. How had his sailing trips continued? Did he get to Norway with his Norwegian passport and French language as he had intended?

What happened to Norman and Monica on the *Charisma* who kept us company for a while along the Atlantic coast of Spain? They had both taken leave from their respective jobs to set off in a boat that was totally unsuitable for long voyages, a light and lively racing yacht, to the stern of which they had lashed two bicycles. When they set sail from Vilagarcía they still had no idea what they would do. Do they know now? And Peter on the *Donclare of Whitby*, probably the most humorous person we ever encountered. We met him as we were sailing into the Caledonian Canal and he was on his way to the Outer Hebrides with his mother on board. He had told her, and asked us to confirm, that the Outer Hebrides were near the Soviet border and that you had to be careful not to get towed away by Soviet submarines. Did they ever reach Barra? And what then? I remember with sadness a skipper from Saluki: Dennis, an elderly gentleman we invited down below into the cramped little cabin on our IF-boat. He arrived in a double-breasted blazer and skipper's cap which he said he had put on as a mark of respect for our voyage across the North Sea in such a small boat. We could not help feeling a glow of pride, because Dennis had sailed half the world in the course of his long life. But the next day we learnt that he had had a heart attack and been rushed to hospital in Glasgow. We never heard whether he survived, or what became of his splendid wooden yacht.

I could go on briefly like this – because it is always hard to recall more than a few cursory details of individual lives – about one person after another. We got to know hundreds of fine characters over the years we were afloat. Most of them we will never meet again. But the memory of those stimulating hours of human warmth and mutual understanding that we spent in their company is something that no one can ever take from us. What did we have in common? Probably a dream, the dream of being able to sail in complete freedom and encounter more of the human and natural world, rendering the question of the meaning of life meaningless.

~

So one meets a lot of people when out sailing for a lengthy period and far away. In itself that may seem strange. Why should we meet more people – and get to know them better – just because of sailing to other countries? The explanation is fairly simple, though twofold. The majority of those who go to sea are seeking new and different experiences. So they make contact more freely and easily, out of interest and inclination. That means of course that those with whom we come in contact are as open to contact as we are ourselves. It is a mutually beneficial circle.

The sad fact is that it is much less often that you get to know the sailors who sit in their boats at their own moorings in their home ports, whether in Limhamn, Dragør, Kinsale, Tréguier or Vilagarcía. You exchange words and superficial greetings, that's all.

But shouldn't a visiting long-distance sailor arriving at your home port be just the kind of person you would want to invite down to your static cabin?

Why not ask: What's happening in America? In Venezuela and Columbia? Well, because you, and we, almost without exception, are a vegetating conventional rabble, too concerned with our own private and self-induced nonsense to remember actively that the Earth is round and has many countries.

(*Cape Farewell*)

What's it like in the world out there? Where have you been? Tell me about the waters you sailed. Did you meet any unforgettable characters? What have you learnt, about yourself, about life? Have you been happy? Could you get by without familiar food? Was it worth the effort of sailing so far? Do you really think we should sail all the way to the Caribbean? Can you drop anchor in the outer skerries of the west coast of Sweden in late autumn in peace and quiet?

But no, you seldom hear questions like these. Curiosity about the foreign and unusual seems to be well concealed in most home-water sailors. If you want to meet people, in the experience of myself and others, you have to seek them among travellers. And among the exceptions, of course, as always.

On fear, anxiety and trepidation

We met Hugh McNair on our very first trip to Scotland. Sten and I had emerged in one piece from Neptune's Staircase, the evocative name of the final set of locks in the Caledonian Canal before you reach the Atlantic Ocean. Behind us in the sea lock was a carrot-coloured steel-hulled yacht of typical home-made design with a lone sailor on board. There was no doubt in our minds that he must be Scottish. With freckles and ginger hair that matched the boat, he needed only bagpipes to complete the picture of the quintessential Scotsman according to our preconceived notions.

Sten and I were vacillating about going through the lock. Partly because there were so many white geese on Loch Linnhe, and partly, and more significantly, because what awaited us beyond the security of the lock gates was an inlet of the Atlantic. It was quite a big step to take for us.

We went over to the carrot-coloured boat, introduced ourselves and asked Hugh, as his name turned out to be, if he had heard the weather forecast. But no, he hadn't.

'If you listened to that too often,' he said, 'you'd never go anywhere.'

We took that reply to mean what the hell, and we may have felt a little ashamed as we went back to the *Moana* after having given Hugh some assistance with the lock and wished him a good passage. He was sailing out completely alone into an onshore gale, while the two of us stood on the quayside dithering.

~

An hour later there was a knock on *Moana*'s coachroof. We put our heads out and saw Hugh's freckled face wearing a slightly embarrassed smile.

'It was blowing quite hard out there,' he said.

That evening we all three sat in *Moana*'s little cabin, drank a couple of glasses of whisky and told the stories of our lives, the way you do when you feel comfortable on a boat and want to get to know one another. Hugh, who was actually only ever called Junior, since he had the same name as his father, said he was a welder by profession and that he had worked a whole year on a North Sea oil-rig, which had given him chronic claustrophobia. He had welded his hull himself with the money he had earned. As far as he was concerned there was only one important thing in life now: to be able to come and go as he pleased. The boat was the means he had chosen, which shows what a symbol of freedom a sailing boat can be. It would have been easy to imagine Junior being put off the sea entirely after having witnessed so many ferocious winter storms on his North Sea oil-rig.

There was only one flaw in Junior's dream of freedom: he could barely sail.

'But,' he said, and meant it, 'if I can manage to get to Glasgow, where I have a good friend, I shall be quite happy.'

Strangely enough, Junior expressed his greatest admiration for us at having dared to sail across the North Sea in an IF-boat. He of all people knew how appalling it could be. Even atop an oil-rig you felt vulnerable and powerless.

What about him, then, we countered, sailing alone without really being able to sail and without even listening to the weather forecast, heading out into the Atlantic without a moment's hesitation, even if he had turned back?

He asked first if we had heard of foolhardiness. Well, in addition to that, he said, fear and anxiety at sea were second nature to him. 'I worry about everything,' he said simply. And he seemed to think that ended the matter.

18

Despite his constant anxiety Junior managed to get himself across the Bay of Biscay and on to Gibraltar. A good while later, we received a postcard from Portugal, on which he wrote that he had stayed longer than intended in Lisbon because of a girl, so long in fact that his coffers had run dry. He had bought a secondhand guitar with his remaining money, taught himself three songs, and had been busking in the street with his ginger hair and freckles. That was what he was like. Even though he worried about everything at sea, there wasn't much that bothered him on land.

The last I heard of him, he was in Gibraltar. He sent a card thanking me for my contribution to the ship's coffers. I had dug out *Rustica*'s spare foreign currency and sent it down to Junior, Poste Restante, Gibraltar.

'This,' I wrote, 'is what I would have put in your hat to hear you play and sing your three songs.'

I have heard no more of Junior since. That's the sad thing about sailing. You meet people who become your friends, only to be separated from them. You try to keep up contact, but as time goes by the connection becomes more and more tenuous until it finally breaks. What is left is just a mental picture, or perhaps at best a photograph with a smile and some freckles, and then nothing. I feel it as a kind of mourning, the impossibility of holding on to all these fleeting but intimate friendships that spring up on our wanderings.

～

In Tréguier, where I had a month on my own, I met John and Lilian. He was a Scot by birth, while Lilian turned out to be a real Dalecarlian from central Sweden, although she had lived in Edinburgh for thirty years. For twenty of those years they had sailed together in Scottish waters. Now, in retirement, they had sold their house, bought a larger boat, a light-blue Biscay 36, and moved on board for good.

Lilian expressed her admiration for Helle's and my crossing of the North Sea, the English Channel and the Irish Sea, just the two of us. She was scared of sailing at night: she was frightened of the dark.

We talked about sailing the west coast of Scotland, because of course I had told them that Scotland was my paradise, despite the weather and the lack of coral reefs and palm trees (well, this last is not quite true, because there are in fact a few palms here and there in southern Scotland, as in Ireland). I asked for tips on safe, secluded and picturesque anchorages. John and Lilian's eyes lit up as they told me of Loch Tarbert. They had sailed there quite recently, out through the sound between Harris and Lewis and then along the coast in a force seven gale to find the narrow inlet to this most beautiful and most desolate bay in Scotland.

'Between Harris and Lewis?' I said. 'But that's the west coast of the Outer Hebrides.'

I couldn't disguise my incredulity. The west coast of the Outer Hebrides must be one of the most exposed places in the world, a lee shore with permanent heavy pounding ocean breakers, few sheltered anchorages and no harbour to seek refuge in when the severe low pressure systems sweep in from the Atlantic. It was a coast to avoid like the plague.

'But how is it,' I asked, 'that you dare sail there, yet you don't dare sail at night?'

They had no real answer to that question, why people can be more afraid of one thing than another, when both are, to say the least, equally dangerous. It hadn't even occurred to them that there was anything odd about it.

~

When Sten and I arrived in Thyborøn in Denmark in the *Moana* after having sailed through the Limfjord with glorious sunshine and favourable winds, Sten was keen to get out into the North Sea and set course for Scotland. The next morning dawned with a strong westerly gale hammering on the beaches and breakwaters. There was a terrifying sea in the Thyborøn channel, looking even worse from our lateral viewpoint on the concrete wall of the fishing harbour.

Sten's eagerness to set off across the North Sea for Scotland quickly evaporated. Our desire, both his and my own, was soon transformed into apprehension when we saw a German-ensigned yacht on its way in through the breaking surf. The boat looked as if it was writhing in agony, rolling and pitching with water streaming over the deck. Twice it took in huge waves over the stern.

Not long afterwards it came into our basin and hove to behind us. A woman sat paralysed in the cockpit while two men tied up very slowly and shakily. When the boat was finally moored the woman burst into tears and the two men sat down and stared into space. They had been so far out on the edge of the precipice that they could not even enjoy the relief of being in harbour.

Sten and I spent five days in Thyborøn while the sea continued to pound on to the beaches and the wind screamed in the rigging. We went to the seamen's club quite a lot, which was full of holed-up fishermen. It was only the biggest trawlers that were still battling their way out into wind and waves in the hunt for catches, so essential if they were to pay off their loans and interest.

I asked some of the fishermen about fear and anxiety, or rather, I asked them when they regarded the weather as so dire or ominous that they wouldn't venture out, or when they would turn their prow to land to seek the safety of harbour. The answers varied, but all were in agreement that it was too risky to go to sea in a violent North Sea gale in winter.

I have read numerous accounts of sailors and fishermen from the old days under sail on voyages from Paimpol or St-Malo in Brittany to the fishing grounds of Iceland or Newfoundland. One-fifth of all sailors used to die at sea during a normal six-month trip. And that was in summer.

Nothing can be further from the truth than to believe that fishermen and other professional sailors are hardened men of the sea. In contrast to most of us amateurs they have a clearer understanding of their limitations. They know when they can no longer manage by their own efforts and when they need help in getting back to port, from luck, chance or what some would call Providence. It is no coincidence that fishing communities in most European countries are among the most religious. Or, for

21

that matter, that fishermen take to the bottle to celebrate having survived another trip. And to forget those who did not come back.

~

There must be carefree sailors, people who don't have the sense to get worried when they see a black thunder cloud on the horizon or hear a gale warning broadcast on the radio when they're out on the open sea. But I incline to think that most of them are inexperienced, unimaginative or hot-headed. A lack of fear and respect for the sea's rage cannot be attributed to anything else.

What can be done, then, to expand your limits, to avoid being so nervous that the trepidation destroys both the experience and the joy in it? What can you do to overcome the fear of sailing at night? How can you rid yourself of the obsession that the North Sea is full of drifting containers? By reference to probability statistics? People who have a fear of flying will be aware that it does not improve matters to know that aircraft are the safest mode of transport of all, even more so than the bicycle. The fact is that there are indeed containers floating around in the North Sea and other oceans. They are difficult to see, and not only at night, because they float exactly level with the surface. The fact is that a fibreglass boat that collides with a container will break its hull. Can we simply ignore facts and pretend there's no danger? Can we? Can our will ever prove superior to fear?

In other words, what can we do to continue to enjoy sailing after having experienced our first violent force eight gale in a small boat on the open sea? What can we do to dispel our fear?

I have no easy answer. But I know that experience and carrying on sailing does not necessarily help.

The Vendée Globe must be one of the toughest races anywhere, a non-stop single-handed circumnavigation of the world. Three months alone in some of the most demanding waters imaginable, the Roaring Forties and the Howling Fifties. Three months *alone* at speeds of twenty knots, half the time in waves over ten metres high, even up to twenty metres, in temperatures dropping below freezing and with the risk of hitting icebergs, night and day. The 1997 race was one of the hardest in a long time. Three boats foundered and one sailor disappeared.

'No words can describe how heavily loneliness weighs,' says Christophe Auguin. 'In prison, even in isolation, there's always a guard the other side of the door. Out in the southern latitudes, thousands of miles from the nearest human being, there are no smells, none of those familiar signs and sounds to indicate that you're not the only living creature on the planet.'

You might think that these lone sailors must be reckless madmen, naïve adventurers, inconsiderate fathers with wives and children ashore exposing themselves to a real risk of death, ungrateful sons and daughters – for women take part as well – leaving their parents in anxious uncertainty for several months a year, that sailing round the world faster than anyone else doesn't prove a thing. You might very well think it would be better for them to risk their lives – if they're going to risk them anyway – for something that would be of benefit to mankind.

That's what you might think. I prefer to admire and be fascinated by people who refuse to believe that the age of adventure is past, who test their limits, who subject themselves to the risk of losing their one and only life. I prefer to try to understand the incomparable experiences, emotions and insights that solo sailors talk about when they come back. 'I want to pursue my dream to the utmost,' says Catherine Chabaud, 'and tell others about this fantastic and unique adventure.'

These adventurous sailing heroes, women as well as men, feel just as much fear as we leisure sailors. It is only their limits that are different. You might think they would get used to it. But no. Loïck Peyron, who won the BOC Challenge, the singlehanded Atlantic race, in 1997, had this to say when he reached harbour:

'I sometimes wonder what the hell I'm doing out at sea. The worst thing about it is that the dread increases with the years. But experience is a tool which it would be a shame not to find a use for. Though in actual fact the ideal sailor would be a complete idiot.'

One of the most gripping novels I know is *The Guns of Navarone*, by Alistair MacLean. The character called Stephens, a young man who became a mountaineer in order to live up to his parents' and others' expectations of resilience and courage, honed his skills to turn himself into one of the best alpinists of his time. The problem was that he could never overcome his fear and anxiety. So, given that he was going to climb, skill was the only cure for his funk. It was from fear of dying on the mountains that Stephens had developed all the qualities necessary to get out of any situation alive. But there was no joy or passion in it for him. Fear, worry, apprehension, anxiety and dread completely spoilt the thrill and excitement of the experience. Only when he was seriously injured on the slopes of Navarone and realised he was going to die did he free himself of his terror and all the other emotions that make life such a torment.

And so it seems to be in reality. The fear of death can be worse than the knowledge that we are going to die. We all know it of course, though we pretend not to.

Serge Gainsbourg, the French troubadour, was once asked how he wanted to die. He replied, in his inimitable style, 'Me? I want to die alive.'

I had a conversation with an old sailor not so long ago, who told me about an atrocious storm in the Bay of Biscay when he was in a small freighter. It had taken them a week and a half to sail from Bordeaux to Cork, a journey that normally took two or three days and nights. Several other bigger ships had gone to the bottom in the same near-hurricane. I asked him whether he had been frightened.

'No,' he said, 'not me. But the mate was at the end of his tether.'

So I wonder, without the least idea myself, why one and not another? For this sailor the storm was an exceptional and magnificent experience, for the mate absolute purgatory. Why? Where do courage and fearlessness come from? Where does the fear of dying come from? I would really like to know.

In July 1996 the French newspaper *Le Monde* interviewed François Mic, a Breton lifeboatman who in the course of his own long life had saved forty-three lives in peril at sea. But who also had failed to save a few lives, people he had watched die before his very eyes, and this embittered his old age and gave him nightmares. He had no time for the romance and poetry of the sea.

'The sea,' he said, 'bides its time, lies in wait, like a crocodile; and swallows all. It is unforgiving. The sea doesn't like human beings. The sea is evil...God, it's evil. How can you love the sea if you are a realist? Why should we romanticise it and describe these dangerous, costly and unnecessary single-handed races as the fulfilment of dreams? Challenge the sea, they say! Just for the honour and the experience! When I challenge the sea, it's to rescue a life from its jaws.'

François Mic is not alone. There are people like him all over the world, people who challenge the sea as unpaid volunteers in order to save the lives of foolish, careless or unlucky seafarers. They are the people who possess real courage, who know how to handle their fear, and who use it to save the only life that each of us is endowed with, while others treat theirs as disposable.

I assume that all the world's military powers have invested large sums – especially dollars – to research the nature of fear and trepidation and attempt to control it. As has been done with sea-sickness, without any effective remedy having been found. I assume too that airlines have pumped considerable resources into investigating our fear of flying. And much money has certainly been spent on eradicating the anxieties that drive people to insanity or suicide.

With rather meagre results, in fact. Neither science nor capital seems to have got the better of mankind's fear and anxiety. Why? There is only one answer as far as I can see: because we are all aware deep down, more or less consciously, more or less subliminally, more or less suppressed, that we only have one life and that's it, that we get no second chance if we die. Those who have a faith and believe in a life after this, whether as paradise or reincarnation, would obviously not agree with me. They are welcome to their beliefs. It is certainly no bed of roses having the conviction that we are only granted one life and that everything we aspire to has to be done in the here and now.

My question to those who believe in an afterlife is this:

Why is it then so sinful to take one's life?

Perhaps because everyone who genuinely believed in paradise in an afterlife would otherwise be tempted to put an end to himself.

~

It is remarkable that Harry Martinson gives no indication in *Aimless Travels* or in *Cape Farewell* that he was afraid, anxious or alarmed during his voyages. Not even when a tornado strikes the timber freighter *Ionopolis* and it is a hair's breadth from sinking does he write of his own fear. He mentions that 'the whole crew fuses into one terrified will: to save the ship and themselves'. Yet it is as if he himself is standing outside of everything. It can sometimes be productive to ask what a person is not. Harry Martinson is *not* sentimental, at least not as an author, at least not as a travel writer. The following morning after *Ionopolis* has lost her cargo he observes:

> Those drowned that night were: Criss Kalliosso from Levkosia, seaman; Aros Cyperin from Paikopolis, chief engineer; and the Belgian deckhand Peter Jan Vrievelde from Adinkerk.

That's all. He then reverts to fantasising about the Captain's wife. Martinson is obviously a kinsman of the old sailor in the Bay of Biscay: cool, calm and collected in the midst of the storm.

I have not read all of Harry Martinson's writings as thoroughly as his travel books, but he is emphatically no chronicler of fear and death.

If I were to make a conjecture, it would be that for anyone brought up an orphan, as Martinson was, death is never entirely real.

And finally: one day I would like to find the drowned sailors' children and grandchildren, nieces and nephews, if there are any. I would like to tell them that they are named by Nobel Prizewinner Harry Martinson in his inimitable *Cape Farewell*. I would like to say to them that a finer obituary and posthumous life could scarcely be imagined.

On dawn

It is four in the morning. I have just taken over the watch and am waiting for the first elusive glimpse of dawn. First light is something you only sense, not that you see. No human eyes can register when night turns into day. Strangely enough it doesn't usually feel as if dawn comes at all. What seems to be happening is that night dissolves and disappears. We may wait eagerly for the first light, the first tone of grey, but we are disappointed when the winking lighthouses and buoys simply lose their brightness and fade.

The darkness of the night is unequivocal and powerful. It is also, when you are used to it, reassuring. We (I) feel uneasy and apprehensive as dawn approaches. At night we are enclosed in a cocoon. There are no ominous stacks of storm clouds to worry about.

This morning the lightening of the skies seems never-ending. The first streak of grey broadens and spreads until everything has acquired the same even hue. There is rain hanging in the air. Visibility may be about one nautical mile, but how can you estimate distance when you can see nothing but greyness, when you can't be sure you're seeing anything at all?

Gradually the feeling of dawn dies away. Nothing to indicate any deterioration in the weather. The dripping sail is filled by a south-westerly breeze and the sea is moderate. Somewhere beyond the mist, perhaps ten nautical miles to leeward, is Ameland, one of the West Frisian islands.

Not a ship in sight, not even a solitary bird. The sea is empty. We, Janne Robertsson and I, are on our way home in *Moana*, an IF-boat. Our last port of call was Den Helder and we are on course for Cuxhaven at the mouth of the River Elbe. We are on our way back; not home, but back. Another hundred and forty nautical miles to sail.

It's a completely ordinary morning in the southern North Sea.

~

Another dawn. The last, we hope, in the Bay of Biscay. Helle and I and *Rustica* are on our way from Belle-Ile, the Beautiful Island, which lives up to its name, to Gijón in Asturias, in the centre of the north coast of Spain. I take over at midnight, in pitch blackness. We have eighty nautical miles to go. A light but variable breeze fills the sails. We're making four knots and steering on autopilot. All is calm and under control on board.

So it continues more or less the same for two hours. I sit around in the cockpit mostly. Half asleep some of the time. Switch on my pocket torch and cast a glance at the compass now and then. Stand up, but only infrequently, to peer out into the darkness just in case, against all expectation, there are any lights on the invisible horizon. Every once in a while I go below and pour myself a drop of coffee and roll a cigarette. I take both up to the cockpit with me. I go down and sit at the chart table, read off our position on the satellite navigation system and enter it on the chart. It was three hours ago when I last did it. On a small-scale general chart like the Bay of Biscay there is no point in marking your position once an hour. It would only serve as a reminder of what slow progress you're actually making.

That's how a night watch passes when all goes well, uneventfully in other words. Quite a comfortable existence, only spoilt by the unremitting weariness and instinctive vigilance. But there is one little source of unease impinging on my consciousness way below the horizon to the south-east: the occasional reflection of lightning discharging from loaded skies. There is a belt of thunderstorms on its way up across France heading for Scandinavia. But if the meteorologists have done their homework, we won't be affected out here.

In the midst of this apparent peace the wind suddenly dies down, not figuratively or relatively, but abruptly and totally. Wind one minute, becalmed the next. The mainsail flaps when the boom starts swinging with *Rustica*'s rolling in the swell. I can just see the jib hanging slack at the bows. I pull in the sheet to silence the mainsail. Unfortunately it's only a partial solution. The way to keep a flapping sail quiet in a swell is to take it down or use the engine and fill the sail by the boat's own motion.

I wait half an hour without feeling the slightest breath of wind. I lift the autopilot off the tiller, because its inbuilt compass has lost all concept of direction. In the end our prow is pointing to France instead of Spain. With a deep inward sigh I decide to start the engine. First I lower the jib and lash it to the lifeline. Then I go below and open the cooling water intake, followed by the discharge valve in the cockpit. Finally I turn the ignition key and give it some throttle. The silence is rent by the diesel engine spluttering into action. I stick my head through the companion-way to alert Helle to what I'm doing, knowing full well that she'll have been woken by the noise. *Rustica* is on course again and the autopilot adjusted to steer us directly to our goal. I'm not entirely happy with the sound of the engine, an incessant cause for concern. I give a few turns to the stuffing box, the grease reservoir for the propeller and propeller shaft, without any noticeable effect. It's probably the oil that needs topping up, but that can wait for a while.

This time it doesn't become relevant. In another half hour the wind returns, though from a different direction, as suddenly as it had died away. When the wind dies, it always feels as if you are becalmed. But when it comes back you always think it's picking you up or coming to meet you. By day, at least. At night, when you can't see the wind on the water, you neither know nor think anything. The wind is suddenly gone. The wind is suddenly back.

Activity on board once more. I go forward and unhitch the jib, go back to the cockpit and hoist it. I switch off the engine with another inward, unexpressed sigh, but this time of relief; relief at not having to listen to the engine-noise, at not having to worry that it doesn't sound as it should.

I close the bottom vents, ease the mainsheet and try to find the angle between the mainsail and the new wind. The same procedure with the jib. Then I connect the autopilot again, before sitting down at the chart table to check our position and enter the events of the last hour in the logbook. When that is all done I roll another cigarette, pour myself half a cup of lukewarm coffee and settle down in the cockpit after making a sweep of the horizon with the binoculars without so much as a glimpse of light. That's when Helle wakes up and starts getting ready to take over.

And people wonder how you occupy your time during long voyages!

No dramatic or significant events, admittedly, but enough to fill a night watch in the Bay of Biscay.

As I sit there with my coffee and cigarette I suddenly discover that I can see. The dawn has overcome the darkness. But I still can't make out the water properly or the crests of the waves; all I can distinguish are leaden masses rising and falling, the ever-present ocean swell. I wait, if not tense, then at least expectant, for what the morning light might reveal. I have to wait quite a while, because the sea that I was hoping would come into view vanishes in a milky haze. This dawn reveals nothing, only fog. Not even ripples on the water, because despite the light wind in the sails the swell is as smooth as glass.

Then the wind gets up and disperses the fog. The swell increases and we head on towards Spain. We sight Gijón at about nine, and a huge ship at anchor in the open sea without the slightest shelter. With a few ifs and buts we tie up in the smart but halfempty EU-financed marina. We are elated and as pleased as Punch to have the Bay of Biscay behind us. But the next stage of the voyage is another story.

∼

It is half past four in the morning. We are somewhere off the coast of Holland, on a south-westerly course, destination St-Malo in Brittany. Janne is fast asleep. It's wet, raw and humid. In the first pale light of dawn it starts to drizzle. Visibility is at most one nautical mile, probably less.

The coffee is scarcely even lukewarm after having stood in the vacuum flask since the previous evening. Cigarettes are hard to roll and taste vile. It would be nice to be in harbour now to have a good sleep, I think with a certain amount of self-pity.

The sea is desolate and deserted. It's as if there are no other people in the world but myself at the tiller and Janne in his berth. And even Janne seems very distant right now.

But I have a sudden feeling that we're not alone. It's not long before I hear the dull throb of a ship's engine. I stare out into the drizzling rain to see where it's coming from. A few minutes later I can make out a dark grey shape to windward, which I immediately recognise as a car ferry bearing down on the *Moana* at full speed. I don't have time for alarm before I see the ferry change course. Is it for our sake? Yes, it would seem so. The ferry passes half a nautical mile astern of us and turns again to resume its previous course. I wave to show my heartfelt thanks and acknowledgement. Did the captain or officer of the watch see us? I have no idea. The ferry vanishes into the mist. Soon it is as if it never existed and we are as alone as before.

Perhaps that is what I remember best about all the dawns I have experienced at sea: the isolation, desolation and the feeling that there is no other world than the one this side of the horizon.

'*The sun rises from the dawn, a flaming golden rose on the bush of the morning cloud*,' Harry Martinson writes in *Cape Farewell*.

Which is exactly how it is.

The sun rises from the dawn. Not vice versa.

Like the dawn itself. It rises out of the darkness, a fleeting and spectral grey silhouette that vanishes without trace into the daylight, as if it had never existed, like the wake of a ship.

On tiredness, relief and joy

I didn't know what tiredness was until I went out into the North Sea for the first time. There were only two of us on board and we had opted for three-hour watches, called Chinese watches, which are draining. We left Zeebrugge early one morning and spent the first night drifting with the current and slack sails somewhere between Dover and Calais. We felt helpless with our meagre four-horsepower outboard motor. The water pulsated beneath the smooth windless surface, heaving, rising and falling, moving round in large masses. Before us lay what looked like an impenetrable line of anchor lights, and we talked about steering out into the Straits of Dover to avoid getting caught up in this net of light. But the rudder wouldn't obey. The seething and majestically swirling currents, like a viscous oil, made us restless and a little anxious. Neither of us felt like sleeping, even if we had been able to. The motor was going for two hours just to keep the bows pointing in the right direction. But it was reassuring.

When morning came the water was normal and it turned out that the cable-laying ships off Cap Gris Nez had left gaps for yachts like the *Moana* to sail through. There are always ships at anchor in the southern North Sea, and they always appear to be in a line, fastened together by their anchor lamps and deck illumination, and right out in the middle of the sea. You imagine you'll get entangled in heavy anchor chains if you try to force your way through.

But you learn (with luck). Off Cap Gris Nez we realised that night vision lacks depth. It has no perspective. Light comes in various strengths, depending on source. It's the same with the stars in the sky. There is no guarantee that the brightest star is the nearest. And so it is at sea. All lights seem to be at the same distance. But they are not. Then again, they may be. But you can't be sure just by eyesight, not even through binoculars.

The next night we lay becalmed. I was kept awake by the mainsheet slapping and the block banging. I knew I had to get some sleep.

The third night descended oppressively in the sultry evening mist off Le Havre without my having had a chance for a proper rest. We were heading for Cap Barfleur, twenty nautical miles east of Cherbourg. Janne woke me at three in the morning just after I had finally managed to drop off. He said he had to call five times before I deigned to answer and let his words penetrate through to my fuddled brain.

I took over the tiller. The first hour passed uneventfully, but then came that infinite tiredness, the sort that seems to divide you in two. A passive body and a consciousness that can only struggle with one thing: staying conscious. At times I couldn't see the compass needle for the flickering in my eyes, even though I knew I was staring at it. Finally, in order not to fall asleep, I made a supreme effort to steer actively and stood up for the rest of my watch. I was several times tempted to wake Janne, but that was the last thing I should do, transfer my exhaustion to him.

When morning came there was the Barfleur lighthouse two compass points to port. In the night mist I hadn't caught even a glimpse of the powerful lamp that according to the chart had a range of twenty nautical miles. But what did that matter now? We knew exactly where we were on the waters of Mother Earth. We could pinpoint our latitude and longitude to within a hundred and fifty metres.

I woke Janne at last. He was pleased to see the lighthouse and I could sense his gratitude to me for doing my bit and steering us so accurately. In these capricious currents a compass and log are not always enough. I told him how I'd had to fight my tiredness and he knew precisely what I meant. We said no more about it.

But what happened to my weariness next? We sailed into Cherbourg's enormous harbour. The outer harbour is so immense that in the heat haze we had to set a course by chart in order not to miss the inner harbour. We put in under sail, which in an IF-boat is not that difficult. Nevertheless there's a special satisfaction in coming into harbour under canvas after a voyage of three nights and three hundred nautical miles. Exhaustion only returned after we had tied up and furled the sails. It swept all before it, even our joy in being so close to our goal. There were only a hundred nautical miles left to St-Malo, to which I had dreamt of sailing in my own boat ever since I had first been there ten years earlier.

~

I felt the same degree of tiredness the following year sitting in a restaurant in the Scottish east coast port of Fraserburgh. I had eaten a meal and drunk a pint of lager. My friend Sten, from Kalvehave in southern Sjælland, and I were celebrating after having crossed the North Sea in three and a half days without mishap.

We had set off from Thyborøn in glorious sunshine and met a rough and choppy swell from the north-west. It was the death-throes of a gale that had been battering the coast of Jutland for forty-eight hours. At about two o'clock I made a meal which may not have been very appetising, but it was edible. It was skipper's lobscouse, one of Sten's favourite dishes, but he only took a few bites before he put down his fork.

Next morning at dawn the inevitable happened: he was seasick. Over the ensuing three days all he ate was a slice of dry bread. On the morning of the second day he looked like living death. I thought of Ian Nicholson's words about seasickness having two stages: the first is when you think you're going to die, the second, and far worse, is when you begin to realise you're not. But it wasn't a joke now. And Nicholson, who himself was always seasick despite his constant sailing, wasn't joking either.

It took Sten three minutes at most to get out of his berth, put on his oilskins, lifejacket and lifeline before he was at the tiller. Any slower and he would have vomited. As I watched him hour after hour battling with himself and the rudder I seriously thought about turning round. We had two reefs in the mainsail and were tacking hard in mountainous seaweed-green waves. But the sun was shining, *Moana* was sailing like a dream, and it was almost as far back to Skagen as it was onward to Scotland.

So we carried on. Sten pulled through and learnt something about himself. On the return passage, two months later, I heard him while he was alone at the tiller, thinking I was asleep, muttering, 'You have to be a masochist to enjoy this.'

He may well have been right. But the strange thing is that despite everything you do somehow 'enjoy it'. Or maybe it's yourself you start to enjoy when you discover that you can endure more than you ever thought possible. A day later, with two hundred nautical miles still to go back to Skagen and home waters, Sten said to me, 'If I've managed this, I ought to be able to manage to give up smoking.'

And so he did, he stopped smoking then and there, in the middle of the North Sea.

But on this last night of the voyage to Scotland he had not yet reached that point. The wind had subsided after blowing hard for forty-eight hours. We were rolling heavily in the old swell. Sten knew I was tired, because I had had to forego some of my three hours' sleep to navigate, eat, reef and generally make myself useful. He sat with the mainsheet in his hand, against all the rules, trying manfully to stop the block banging like a pistol shot against the traveller. But I woke up several times anyway.

When I was finally sound asleep Sten woke me deliberately. I didn't even ask what he wanted, just got up mechanically and looked out into the darkness. To port, on a collision course, I saw the hundreds of lights of what must have been an oil-rig. Strange, I thought, dulled by lack of sleep, because here, a hundred nautical miles east of Rattray Head, the sea should have been empty.

'It must be the current,' said Sten. 'I've been trying to steer us clear of it, but it's getting closer all the time.'

Weird, I thought again, sluggishly. Out here the current should be negligible. It was Sten himself who solved the riddle.

'Maybe it's the rig that's moving, and not us.'

I whipped out the binoculars. Then I saw what it was: an oil-rig being towed right across our path at a speed of more than ten knots by a tug as big as a car ferry. The tug and the eleven storey high platform passed in front of us half a nautical mile ahead. Great was our relief.

~

The same tension and relief the year before. We were on our way to Zeebrugge, sailing down the Dutch coast. I was on watch and saw another illuminated 'Christmas tree' that was not marked on the chart. A new boring rig, I thought, and told Janne when he took over that he ought to keep well clear of it.

An hour later I was woken by Janne asking me to hand him the lamp as he squinted out into the darkness. He grabbed it and shone it over the bows. Right on our course, about thirty metres ahead, was a huge unlit lump of concrete being used as a mooring for ships delivering supplies to the rig. Janne veered away and gave me back the lamp. I could see he was shaken. He couldn't sleep any more that night. The danger had been too close for us even to feel any relief when it was discovered and avoided.

In fact it was the second incident on that voyage along the coast of the southern North Sea. A few days earlier I had been on watch and had checked the numerous vessels on course towards us a nautical mile to starboard in the shipping lane marked out for deep-draught steel colossi. I had just confirmed that they were all keeping to their lanes as they should and was concentrating on the compass; I didn't want us drifting off course into the shipping lane.

Looking out under the genoa ten minutes later I saw to my consternation a ship bearing straight down on us. I had to wake Janne and tell him to put on his lifejacket. Just saying the words felt unreal. We gybed twice in the hope of getting someone on their bridge to notice our lamps. Only three hundred metres separated us when the ship suddenly yawed away and sailed back out to the deep-water channel where it belonged.

Someone must have been asleep on watch and let it wander off course. It could have been a catastrophe for us.

Sten and I had no such worries on our way to Scotland. The North Sea was wonderfully free of ships and we saw no oilfields. There was nothing but sea and yet more sea.

Just before dawn on the last night Sten woke me. It was my turn on watch. The wind had returned, a light following breeze from the south-east. Broad reach with filled sail. Splendid.

As dawn broke the sun rose over the horizon behind the sea we would soon have traversed. The dampness that always condenses in the air at night was slowly drying out. I lay back in the cockpit and relaxed. The wind was freshening up and we were making six knots through the water. I tried to stop myself scanning the horizon for land. By my dead reckoning there were still sixty nautical miles to go. Ten hours at this speed. I cheered *Moana* on, silently, so as not to wake Sten, when the log-line touched on the figure seven.

In the arrogance of my pleasure I let him sleep through the change of watch. There were only seven hours to go till we should sight land. But without my really noticing it the wind had risen. By the time Sten woke at about ten o'clock we had a strong south-easterly which was still increasing. The crests of the waves were getting ever higher and the troughs ever deeper. We lowered the jib and lashed it on deck. The waves were getting steeper and steeper, a sure sign that we were coming close to land.

Suddenly, at the top of a wave, I saw a pale streak and the next second a lighthouse. It was Rattray Head, the very lighthouse I had been setting course for ever since we left Thyborøn, 380 nautical miles behind us. We had made thirteen changes of course, sailed for three days and three nights, and still hit a bullseye, with nothing but log and compass, as if we had only sailed from Limhamn to Dragør. I couldn't help a slight sense of pride.

But I had no time to revel in it. The waves were bigger and steeper than any I'd ever seen. At times we were planing so that the log hit the limit at ten knots. The crests of the waves were breaking over us and looked as if they wanted to swallow us hook, line and sinker. It was worse for

Sten standing in the companionway and seeing them rolling towards us. To give him something to do I asked him to take photographs. I had no great desire myself to turn round and see the walls of water rearing up and hollowing out as if they were a maw on the point of devouring us. I only needed to look at Sten's face to know when another monster was on its way. But every time *Moana* rose up and glided over them. We took in not a single drop of water over the stern.

Then I realised that the current had swept us south and we would have to gybe to get round Rattray Head and into Fraserburgh. It wasn't a very comfortable feeling to have to gybe so close to a lee shore with full mainsail in a force seven or eight gale blowing at up to forty miles an hour. But at least I had swapped the rigging wire for a thicker size, so thick that the rigging supplier had laughed at me and asked whether I was intending to 'make a Greenland turn', meaning to slew round as if I were in a kayak instead of an IF-boat. I was glad now that I had stuck to my guns. I waited till we speeded up on an extra large wave, but despite our own surge forward taking some of the wind pressure out of the sail, it cracked like a whip when sail and boom changed sides. But everything held. And I knew that we still had a margin to spare, even if not much of one.

∼

You shift the boundaries all the time when sailing. The previous year we had been in Cherbourg waiting for gentler winds for the 215 nautical miles that lay between us and Dunkirk. Strong winds were forecast and we were hesitant about venturing out into the Channel. I went over to an English gentleman we had met on Guernsey and asked him what he thought about the wind and weather. He opined that the wind was too strong for us to enjoy the sailing anyway. Yachting, he said, should be fun, not masochism. And when I turned to go, none the wiser, he said, 'I do hope you won't sail!'

But we risked it and made sixty nautical miles in eight hours in the strong wind and favourable current. A few hours before dusk the wind got up even more and we knew we should have followed the Englishman's advice. The sun lay like a glowing orb on the horizon, but we only saw it intermittently. In the troughs it disappeared completely. Those well-versed in trigonometry could have calculated from that the actual size of the waves, but for the three of us, Janne, Helle and myself, it was enough to know that they were big enough to block out a glowing sun on the horizon. Every other wave made the log hit the limit. It's simultaneously elating and unpleasant doing ten knots in a long-keeled boat like the *Moana*. At one point I couldn't believe my eyes. Our bow wave was right back at the sheet winches by the cockpit, just as if we were water ski-ing. When we were at the bottom of the trough the wave collapsed and threw no more than a bucketful of water over the rail.

We had to reduce our speed. We decided to take down the small jib. We were right in the shipping lane and had to be able to keep out of the way of vessels looming up astern all the time like ghosts. Some of them actually altered course. Whether because they saw our reflector on their radar or our masthead light swaying backwards and forwards was impossible to determine. We didn't say much, but I think we all knew that our margins had narrowed. Everything was fine so far, but we couldn't afford anything to give way under the strain.

I handed over to Helle at ten o'clock and tried to sleep. But I hadn't been lying in the forepeak long when I heard a strange booming noise that seemed to be coming from every direction and filling the whole boat. Then the roar of a colossal wave breaking behind us for as far as we could see. And a splashing sound and a shout from Helle. We were lucky. The worst of its power was already spent when the wave hit *Moana*'s stern, giving the terrified Helle a soaking.

Our feeling of vulnerability was not aided by the fact that the horizon ahead was illuminated by lightning from a tremendous thunderstorm somewhere between Dover and Calais. Navigation was becoming very approximate. Radio direction finders are unreliable at dusk and in rough seas. There were no harbours within reach for us to shelter in. The pilot manuals warned explicitly against approaching them in strong westerlies.

'*Our one piece of luck was that we were on the high seas,*' Harry Martinson writes in *Cape Farewell*, and for once sounds almost guilty of cliché. But in fact it's only a hackneyed phrase for landlubbers. No literary style could ever disguise the fact that the most dangerous aspect of being at sea is proximity to land.

So as not to implant any false hopes I said we might as well continue out into the North Sea, as far as Cuxhaven if necessary, till the gale had blown itself out. The decision gave us an injection of fortitude.

It blew hard all night. We didn't know how hard. I fell asleep in the end, while Janne and Helle took care of *Moana*. When they woke me at four o'clock, soon after dawn, everything was different. The sun was shining, the thunderstorm had passed and we could scarcely feel the wind. The white chalk cliffs of Dover were gleaming to the north-east. To the south-east Cap Gris Nez was outlined razorsharp against the early morning sun.

I heard from the others that it had not been an easy night. At one in the morning Helle had listened to the shipping forecast from the BBC and was treated to a gale warning, force eight, which is over forty miles an hour. Janne said afterwards that he could see from Helle's face, before she said a word, that it was likely to get worse. But it didn't. Gale force eight was what we were already experiencing.

Helle and Janne went to lie down and I steered us on towards Dunkirk. The sun was hot and I marvelled at how rapidly everything can change at sea. At the same time I saw how our limits shift: everything is relative. We were still doing five knots with only a double-reefed mainsail, but compared with how it had been, there seemed to be virtually no wind at all.

When we put in to Dunkirk at two o'clock we poured ourselves a well-deserved whisky and exchanged glances. We didn't say much then either. There was nothing to say that we didn't already know. We uttered a few words about how difficult it would be to get someone else to understand what we had been through.

It was exactly the same emotion that Sten and I had the following year when we finally sailed in between Fraserburgh's gigantic breakwaters, built to withstand the northerly storms that have a free run from the Arctic to Scotland. We were suffused with the warm glow of having arrived and having achieved what we set out to do, but were sparing with our words. We had nothing to say after the last few hours sailing in such terrible waves. I had been convinced for a while that we wouldn't be able to enter Fraserburgh's east-facing harbour. I told Sten we might have to do another fifty nautical miles and saw his face crumple. But when we came round Rattray Head we were sheltered from the open sea and able to put into port, a tiny speck of a boat among all the gigantic ocean trawlers. The fact that we were able to get in at all intensified our joy all the more, of course, when we finally stood in the drizzle and mist looking up at Fraserburgh's grey granite architecture.

The next day there was a ceremony in the harbour. The Duke of Kent had come to launch the new lifeboat. It was the third the town had had, and the first for many years, since the previous two had capsized with all hands in the very waters where we had encountered such rough steep seas. I read later in the Cruising Club handbook a special warning for the area around Rattray Head in easterly gales. If anything had happened to the *Moana* and us it would have been my fault for not doing my homework. Which is inexcusable.

But I have seldom experienced such tranquillity as when we came back to the boat and bedded down after pub and restaurant. Just knowing that I didn't need to get up again three hours later made all other paradises pale into insignificance.

We slept for six hours. Then at four o'clock in the morning we were both woken by noises on deck. We got up in sprightly fashion. The thought of being able to go back to sleep for all eternity made waking up a solace for the soul. Happiness for both a sailor and a tramp can be something as simple as being able to go back to sleep at will. When we came up on deck we found fishermen padding around re-tying the boat so that they could put out to sea themselves. They waved us away when we appeared.

'We'll take care of this. Go back to sleep!'

It would have been worth sailing across the North Sea just to hear those words.

'*It is good to have a lantern*,' Harry Martinson writes on his walk through Brazil. '*Better and more heart-warming than owning a big house. Good to wander like this with a lantern through the forests of Brazil.*'

(*Cape Farewell*)

That's all it takes to make a nomad happy.

On explaining the inexplicable

After nine months sailing and wintering in Ireland we set off from Kinsale early one misty morning. We had known for a week that it was time to move on from Ireland, where we had lived such a good life. Curiosity and wanderlust had finally got the better of us. Yet it was still sad to leave Kinsale and the friends we had acquired, rather than made, for in Ireland people in general seem to be friendlier and more forthcoming than in most other places, at least in Europe, at least in the countries of Europe that I am familiar with. When will we next meet Mary of the Tap Tavern, our local pub? When will we next hear Björn and Barbara's infectious laughter and enthusiasm? And diffident Giles, the harbourmaster – will we ever bump into him again? Captain John in his old wooden boat? The ship's boy on *Silver Tara*, simply called 'the Kiwi' because he was a New Zealander? Tony, the travel agent, who one day drove me round half of County Cork just to show me part of his beloved Ireland? Or Michael, who played guitar in the pub, will we ever see him again?

None of them was up and about, of course, when we made such an early start in the hope of reaching Newlyn in Cornwall before dark the next day. Only one solitary soul was awake, and that was almost worst of all. John, from the steel-hulled *Abba* that had wintered with us, stood alone on the quay. His sorrow was great. Having lived on board for fifteen years, his wife had persuaded him to move ashore. They had bought a little cottage in the south of England.

But in his heart John didn't want to. Jokingly he said that he never should have sailed the west coast of Ireland the year before. 'That took two years off our life expectancy.'

What he meant was that the voyage was so difficult and stressful that his wife was deterred from any more sailing. He stood there now waving us off, in the knowledge that no one would ever again come do the same for him. That is hard to bear.

~

This was not to be about loss, but about the inexplicable. Although maybe this passion of John's for his boat and the sea, this urge to live and travel in a slender curved box, is also ultimately inexplicable.

Later that day after taking our leave of Kinsale our engine failed. That at least was not inexplicable, given its age. Our first thought was to turn back for repairs, but while we were pondering the wind got up and we decided to sail on. After all, we had sailed solely under canvas for several years, even if not in such capricious and treacherous waters as the Irish Sea.

Late in the afternoon we were making fair speed in a light breeze on an empty sea in warm sun. Seabirds were our only company, big yellow-billed gannets and grey gulls. They were beautiful to watch, but not particularly communicative. As raucous and noisy as herring gulls are ashore or round fishing boats, they are totally silent at sea. Helle and I sat dozing in the cockpit. The weather forecast was excellent. The Irish Sea was going to be on its best behaviour overnight.

All of a sudden our peace and quiet was shattered by two almighty explosions, like cannon fire. Thousands of seabirds rose in the air squawking and screeching louder than you'd have thought them capable of out there. It was some minutes before they lapsed into silence and touched down again. We scanned the horizon, even through binoculars, but the sea was just as empty and virginal as before.

What could it have been? Naval vessels beyond the horizon? The bangs were too sharp. Military aircraft on exercises? Then we would have heard the noise of their jet engines.

We let the question rest. What else could we do? We had no choice. Other than to endure the uncertainty.

~

We rounded Land's End the next day in evening mist, and no sooner had we done so than the wind died and we could feel warm gusts off the land. There was thunder in the air. We managed to start the engine, but it sounded so feeble and strained that we didn't dare risk running it for more than a short while, enough to get us past a green buoy so that we could set course into the bay where, behind the point, Newlyn lay concealed. To our great relief the wind returned, but now from the bay. We began to tack as darkness fell. It soon developed into a fresh breeze and the water was splashing up over the sprayhood in the choppy seas. We had our hands full, one of us sailing, the other navigating and trying to identify all the lights on land. It was one of those situations where the adrenalin flows without there being any real danger. The problem that evening was that Helle and I couldn't agree on what we saw. How many flashes? Did you see that buoy? Do you think that's the harbour entrance? And so on and so forth.

Then suddenly in the midst of all this natural uncertainty we heard an extraordinary noise somewhere behind us. We turned round and what did we see? A bright sparkling red light apparently suspended a couple of hundred metres above the water. It was moving slowly from side to side and up and down, making a swishing sound that blended with the whistle of the wind into something quite bizarre. It wasn't a ship, that much was certain. Nor a plane. We had seen enough of them when wintering in Dragør to be able to identify them in the dark. The object seemed at times to be coming closer, then to recede, sometimes to stop and quiver in one place.

But we had to navigate and keep our eyes on where we were. We couldn't spare time for the strange and inexplicable. Yet even while Helle was giving me courses to steer it was still on my mind. In the end I thought I had it. 'A helicopter,' I said. 'It must be a helicopter.'

I had remembered that there was something about helicopter exercises on the chart. That must be it. But I couldn't be sure. There was no incontrovertible evidence.

~

Long afterwards I mentioned the bangs out in the Irish Sea to someone who was convinced it must have been a Concorde breaking the sound barrier on its way across the Atlantic. I believed it because it could explain the inexplicable. Can I know for certain that these were the solutions, the one a supersonic plane and the other a helicopter? No, of course not, but what can we do except take probability as a reasonable guess at the truth if we want to avoid filling our heads with fanciful notions?

A German linguist, Scheler, has rightly pointed out that man abhors a semantic vacuum, which is to say that one of the worst things that can happen to a person is not to understand or be understood. The psychologist Frankl, after his experiences in the concentration camp at Buchenwald, wrote thousands of pages demonstrating that one of man's strongest urges, as powerful as sexuality or self-preservation, is the search for meaning: the will and desire to understand and be understood. I have written a good three hundred pages myself arguing that man's greatest discovery was the invention of meaning based on symbols, that something can stand in the place of something else.

Is there anything worse than the feeling of meaninglessness?

And tragically enough, isn't this feeling more widespread nowadays than ever?

Isn't it to find meaning in an otherwise unintelligible existence that so many people fall victim to all kinds of gurus, to astrologers and cults, to fortune-tellers and prophets, to gods and idols?

In bygone days, long before our present sophisticated electronic navigation instruments, with which we can determine our position within a few metres, people navigated by dead reckoning. This meant navigating by nothing more than course and speed. Competent navigators knew that a position calculated by dead reckoning became increasingly unreliable the further the distance from the starting point. Drift and current were difficult to calculate with any precision, and estimated error accumulates. A position based on dead reckoning is therefore always drawn as a circle. And the further you sail, the bigger the circle. The intelligent navigator takes account of the uncertainty and keeps himself aware of it by making his circles bigger and bigger, is prepared for anything to happen near the edge of the circle, and never indulges in wishful thinking by imagining that his vessel is safely in the centre of the circle rather than on its vulnerable periphery.

So at sea people were forced to live in uncertainty. At sea it was more dangerous to think you knew too much than too little. At sea you had to put the inexplicable in parenthesis, to put your search for meaning aside, to let the inexplicable remain inexplicable without becoming preoccupied by it.

Where on land do you learn that nowadays? It is frequently said that 'the more you learn, the less you know'. But even if that were true in any way, there are not many who take it seriously.

Paradoxically, though we apparently know more and more nowadays, we seem at the same time to have an ever greater need of faith. Not long ago the French weekly *L'Express* had a special issue devoted to astrology. They reported that in France alone there were ten thousand astrologers making a living from their profession, that forty per cent of all Frenchmen read their horoscopes at least once a week, and that one in ten companies used astrologers to select the most suitable applicant for a post.

What we have to ask ourselves is why we have to believe anything at all about things of which we are ignorant. Why do we find it so hard to live with uncertainty? Why are there so few who dare to live by dead reckoning?

But I am still subject to my own wishful thinking and search for truth. For Harry Martinson was so right, so right when he said:

A lot of fantasies are born at sea, and they can overwhelm a cabin-boy

who is little more than a child. They thrive and flourish as a frisson
of fear against a backdrop of curling coal smoke and blue-black
thunder-clouds.

(Cape Farewell)

Right, so right: it is true that superstition and credulity, coins under the
mast and a prohibition on whistling, have filled all the ships in the world
with both comfort and fear.

So where is the truth to be found?

Those who seriously dare to live their lives by dead reckoning, at sea or
on land, can probably be counted on the fingers of one hand.

On happiness

What is it that instils such a feeling of happiness when you have moored up in a new harbour after a long crossing? I have seldom been so happy, so deeply contented, as when Janne and I sighted the walls of St-Malo in early morning mist, or when we sailed into Brunsbüttel lock to enter the Kiel Canal on the way home after having been hove to all night off the mouth of the River Elbe, in an almighty thunderstorm, waiting for the tide to turn. Or as happy and contented as when Sten and I shook hands in Fraserburgh after our North Sea crossing, or when we sailed into Aalbæk on the northern tip of Jutland after 480 nautical miles non-stop from Buckie in Scotland, having ripped our mainsail a few cable-lengths from the harbour entrance. Or when I came into Fraserburgh the second time after Helle and I had scudded towards land in the most fearsome seas and darkness and sailed in between the huge moles just before it blew a real gale. And when afterwards, with the whole cabin full of drenched charts and oilskins, we rang the coastguard in Aberdeen to report as we had promised out at sea that we were safe and sound in harbour. Or when after twenty-four sleepless hours we put into Tréguier after crossing the English Channel and ran to the baker's to buy our first baguette before it closed.

There may be an explanation for the untrammelled gratification I experienced as we approached St-Malo. It was in St-Malo that my dream of sailing began.

Even though I have no geographical roots, there is one place where I have felt at home, and that is St-Malo – at least in the winter when the tourists stay away. The walled granite city and its inhabitants are entirely turned towards the sea, only joined to the mainland by a narrow, artificially constructed tongue of land. St-Malo is really an island, not, as you might think today, an extremity of the mainland. Within the city walls you are both enclosed and protected – St-Malo is one of the few towns that no one had succeeded in taking before the Germans in the Second World War – but from the ramparts you can see out over the world.

The Malouins have been orientated towards the world beyond the horizon throughout the ages. It was they who discovered Canada. It was they who first set foot on the Islas Malvinas, as the Falkland Islands are called in Spanish, islands that at the beginning were neither British nor Argentinean, but Malouin. No one mentioned this during that absurd war.

It was also the Malouins who equipped the largest fleets for fishing off Newfoundland, or Terre Neuve. Hundreds of sailing ships would set off every year for the northwest and the shoals of cod. They would come back home six months later fully laden with salted fish that brought enormous profits to the ship-owners. The loss every season of hundreds of sailors drowned or otherwise killed didn't seem to have any detrimental effect on the financial accounts. And every year the ships took on new crews and sailed off over the horizon.

Even today the Malouins defy the constraints of their walls by travelling. All the ones I know talk of wanting to travel, of having to travel, yet they never get far because they always come back. I have seldom met so many who are so torn between the desire to get away and the desire to stay at home.

In other words it was only natural that it should be in St-Malo that I began to dream of sailing. I was infected by the wanderlust that I saw in their faces and which seemed permanently etched into the walls and quays. Summer after summer I stood on the ramparts looking out over the Atlantic. In Paris, where I was living, I devoured boating magazines and books about round-the-world voyages. In Copenhagen, where I moved next, I met Helle, who gave me the courage to purchase my first boat, which was the Folkboat *Skum*, number 38, built in 1943, with no engine but with oars and rowlocks, as in the original specifications for its class.

When I started sailing the *Skum* I knew more about wind and waves round Cape Horn than about hoisting the mainsail or sheeting the jib. But that first summer was tailor-made for beginners. A sea breeze by day that dropped in the afternoon when we came to enter a new and unfamiliar harbour under sail. Without power you have no choice but to learn to sail. Or tire and give up.

I was lucky and was not scared off. On the contrary, my appetite was whetted and my dreams became more ambitious. For me, a boat was, and still is, a tool in the service of freedom. A small inheritance enabled me to change to an IF-boat. Not that it was a better boat, but the *Skum* didn't have a self-draining cockpit. And even though I was prepared to pay a certain price to realise my dreams, losing my head, in either sense, is not one of them. I also installed an extra self-draining device on the *Moana* and strengthened the rigging.

The second summer with *Moana* and my fourth season as a barely proficient sailor, we set out from Kalvehave in southern Jutland, Janne Robertsson, Helle and myself. Destination: St-Malo.

On the final night of the passage, the hundred nautical miles from Cherbourg to St-Malo, we all stayed awake. We sped through the Alderney Races, or Raz de Blanchard, as they're called in French, just before dusk, in calm and hazy weather.

We sat up the whole night talking beneath the stars. We had an uninterrupted view above us, but the haze hid everything all around. We didn't see the lighthouses on Jersey, only a few nautical miles away, at all. But what did it matter when our upward view extended into the heavens?

Janne and I probably talked about concrete. That may sound strange, but the fact is that we often discussed concrete on night watch. He is an architect and I don't like concrete. So we compared concrete walls in Lund and Stockholm to try to understand why our opinions differed so radically. We didn't arrive at any conclusion, as far as I remember. But then I'm not entirely sure that the point of our conversation was actually to solve anything.

At hourly intervals through the night I would sit down over the charts and plot tide vectors. I was familiar with the theory of tides and currents, while Janne was the practical man who turned the dial and aerial of the radio direction finder.

We kept a lookout for the lighthouse at Cap Fréhel, immediately to the west of St-Malo. It should have been visible at a distance of forty nautical miles, but we didn't see it until it revealed itself out of the mist at dawn on the top of its 200-foot-high cliff half a nautical mile ahead. We 'turned left' as we so nonchalantly put it, and were suddenly among the hooting buoys in the channel to St-Malo. Island after island emerged from the mist, many with ruined castles or fortifications that looked as if they were straight out of *The Count of Monte Cristo*. We met a pilot boat on its way out to sea, and the pilot waved. Perhaps the Swedish flag looked exotic and alien, especially on such a tiny yacht. That's what we liked to think, anyway.

And then the rooftops of St-Malo appeared above its encircling wall. I was as happy as a child on Christmas Day. I accepted it as quite normal that we should arrive precisely at high tide so that we entered the lock to the inner harbour after only a quarter-hour wait. The difference between high and low water in St-Malo is twelve metres on a full tide. If you arrive at low tide you can have a very long wait before going through the lock.

As soon as we had moored I went up into town. I breathed in familiar smells and found my bearings. Yet St-Malo felt quite different this time. My heart was thudding as I approached the office where Yann and Véronique Cayré worked, my good friends with whom I had always stayed over the years. I opened the door.

Yann was used to my turning up unannounced, but his smile nevertheless betrayed a hint of surprise. This time I had not given them an inkling that I might be on my way to St-Malo.

'Whereabouts have you come from?' he asked.

'Cherbourg.'

'Cherbourg?'

'Yes, and before that Cuxhaven, Zeebrugge and Dunkirk. I've sailed here.'

It took a moment before Yann realised I was telling the truth. He had never really believed in my fantasies of one day sailing to St-Malo in my own boat. When we last met I hadn't even been able to sail.

That was one of the best moments of my life, without compare. Why? Just because I had sailed there? Was that so remarkable? I had fulfilled other dreams on land without being on cloud nine like this. I can't explain it, but I know I'm not alone in having such feelings of elation. Other sailors have them too. And they probably find it just as hard to believe as I do that you can feel the same satisfaction and happiness in the same pure and unadulterated form on dry land.

I experienced it when Sten and I sailed into Aalbæk harbour after 480 nautical miles at sea and intermittent bad weather. Is it the distance that counts? The vulnerability? Adversity overcome and exhaustion after five days and nights on three-hour watches?

Not entirely, for this time we had already got our second wind, so to speak, and were in that state when you feel you can carry on sailing for ever. Yet we had had long periods of atrocious weather conditions. For two of the five days we sailed with two reefs in our mainsail and a little Folkboat jib. I don't know what it was blowing, but we kept up an average speed of five and a half knots, which is a lot for an IF-boat.

We tied up alongside a Swedish yacht. Sten and I had both caught up on our sleep and I had spent the last few hours cleaning and tidying before we made harbour. The skipper of the neighbouring boat asked innocently where we had come from. I can't deny a certain self-gratification in being able to reply, 'From Buckie,' and to hear his response, 'Where's that?'

Later on we invited them aboard for a drink of the best malt whisky, brought with us direct from the Scottish Highlands. It was a divine whisky that couldn't be purchased in Denmark for less than £40 a bottle. Sten and I gave one another a despondent look when we saw our Swedish guests empty their glasses and expect a refill.

We were home again. The fleeting happiness of arrival soon slips through our fingers, unfortunately.

Yet we never arrive at our destination to taste that elusive morsel of happiness, for it flees ahead of us in terror because the devil is riding us so hard.

(*Cape Farewell*)

That is where settled householders make their mistake.

'*He appears as full of magic as a troll*,' Harry Martinson writes, of a watchman in a British industrial harbour. '*But don't believe it. His head is full of common sense. Four plus four are eight. Wool grows on sheep, not on trees. And the North Sea is simply water.*'

It is not easy to hold on to happiness when surrounded by people who are nothing but rationality and common sense.

On lessons for life and tests of manhood

Can we learn anything valuable or indispensable about life from a small sailing craft on the open sea? Anything that we cannot experience elsewhere or in any other way?

I would like to think so, of course. But I also have to admit that the lessons to be learnt do not come automatically.

Our vulnerability, for example. Or our insignificance when confronted by a towering sea foaming with rage.

In contrast to all those – including Shakespeare – who have asserted that man is no more than a puff of wind, a speck of fly-dung, the French philosopher Pascal contended that man is like a reed. When tempests rage, he gives way, bends aside, but straightens up unbroken, while the haughty tree splits asunder or is uprooted. What is the truth about us human beings? At sea there are those who give way and straighten up again, those who succumb to panic and break down, those who grapple and fight, but manage to ride out the storm. No, there are few truths about us that cannot be countered by their opposite.

Should the sea not be a source of humility? Yes, it *should* be. But there are nevertheless some who survive its dangers who talk big. They want it known that they emerged victorious from the struggle, that they conquered the sea, when the only victory they can possibly claim is over themselves. Boris Vian, the French author and musician, put his trumpet finger on the nub of the matter when he remarked that soldiers who survived a war were always inclined to believe that the war hadn't been that bad. And where do we frequently find the most belligerent aggressors, the biggest loudmouths, if not among former soldiers, war veterans, the very ones who *ought* to know better? But don't.

Another Frenchman, the Breton singer Bernard Lavilliers, says in one of his poignant lyrics that 'there are three kinds of people, the dead, the living and those who sail the seas'.

It is an attractive thought. But is there any truth in it? We can gain an infinite amount of wisdom from the sea and from sailing, alone or with others. But we can also, it seems, learn nothing, just put on our blinkers and go ashore unchanged.

What is it, then, that we can gain from our intimacy with the sea in a small boat, if we have both the desire and the right attitude? Erskine Childers, the Irish author of *The Riddle of the Sands*, seems to me to have expressed part of the answer. In one of his articles about sailing in *The Times* in the early 1900s he asks himself what it can be that drives 'persons of regular habits and settled tastes, prudent, fastidious and punctual', to set off in small boats and expose themselves to all the discomforts and hazards of the sea. His answer is that 'something has been conquered, not only by power but by love; the world has grown to double its old dimensions, and is seen for the first time in harmony. New values have established themselves upon the wreckage of old standards of utility and gratification'.

~

'New values have established themselves upon the wreckage of old standards of utility and gratification.' Those are no small demands that Childers is making of the wisdom the sea can impart. The key words are love and harmony, with a trace of the mystery of existence.

In another article it is man's battle with himself that can give the sailor unforgettable experiences and knowledge unattainable in any other way:

At bottom, of course, the explanation of its charm for the few lies

57

in the very circumstances which condemn it for the many: in the stark loneliness of the conflict with a formidable element, in the voluntary abnegation of all human aid, moral or physical, and in the submission of a man's own faculties to a merciless ordeal, self-imposed, self-contemplated. Nobody is looking on; if there is no ridicule for blunders, there is no applause for triumphs. Without a rival to vanquish or a tribunal to satisfy, save that of a man's own soul, the competitive and spectacular elements inherent in most sports are totally absent. Absent too, except for rare and brief intervals, is the sense of recreation pure and simple. Body and brain are continually at high tension. Emergency succeeds emergency, and you are exceedingly lucky if one can be dealt with before the next is on you. Often they accumulate until they produce a situation so complex that there seems to be no solution. But the rude schooling of necessity ripens capacity and sharpens the senses amazingly.

(A Thirst for the Sea: The Sailing Adventures of Erskine Childers. Edited by Hugh & Robin Popham. London: Stanford Maritime, 1979.)

There is much food for thought here. But what can Childers mean by saying that sailing is never, except for very brief moments, pure and simple recreation? Does sailing in a little boat always involve fear and anxiety, tension and concentration, problems and incidents? Is it really true that you can never relax and surrender yourself to the beauty of the sea without thinking about the next manoeuvre or an imminent change in the weather? Can we not be transported by the splendour of a cloud formation without simultaneously assessing its height, movement and colour shifts to predict the wind beneath it?

It depends of course on where you sail. But in Ireland, which is three-quarters surrounded by the Atlantic Ocean, it is not often you can relax and forget where you are. Every time you nose your prow out of a sheltered anchorage you meet the ocean. Every time you want to sail even a few nautical miles to the next bay you have to prepare the boat as if for an Atlantic crossing.

Brittany, at least on the north and west coasts, is even worse with its swirling tides. Sailing along the north coast of Spain means sailing along the coast of the Bay of Biscay, some of the most infamous waters in the world. In Scotland there are straits like Corryvreckan and Pentland Firth, through which only madmen would sail with gay abandon.

There is a tendency among sailors to think it a greater achievement to sail across the Atlantic than to cross the North Sea or the Baltic. A round-the-world yachtsman is treated with more respect than one who has navigated the coast of Norway or ridden out a storm in the Kattegat. But courage, endurance and seamanship have nothing to do with distance.

If you want to prove to yourself and to others what an expert you are, you might as well start from Thyborøn on the North Sea coast: wait till it's blowing a full gale and then set out along the coast for a day or two. Even the Kattegat would suffice if you want to put your seamanship to the test or play maritime Russian roulette. The Kattegat is a challenge easily on a par with more open waters. After only six hours of storm the waves reach their maximum height ten nautical miles from the lee shore. This maximum height is – imagine this – seventeen metres! That is why even large ships anchor in the Öresund or in Pakhus Bay on the south side of the island of Anholt in foul weather. Add to the equation the fact that land is always menacingly close; you can't just take down all the sails, batten down the hatches, let yourself be driven by wind and waves and hope that all will be well, regardless of what gods you pray to. Sooner or later, most probably sooner, you'll be swept by westerly winds on to the granite cliffs of Kullen Point on the Swedish coast at the southern end of the Kattegat, or aground on the skerries off Falkenberg further up the west coast of Sweden and smashed to pieces. And the waves in the Kattegat, as in the Baltic, are much shorter and steeper than out in the Atlantic.

It is simply that there is not so much prestige in having battled with a storm in the Kattegat as in having sailed round the world with warm tradewinds behind you. Quite the contrary: anyone who just sailed out into the North Sea in a storm for the fun of it would be regarded as insane. With good reason! But that doesn't alter the fact that all seas, including the Baltic and the Kattegat, are bigger and stronger than the people who sail them, whether it be in a small yacht, a passenger ferry like the *Estonia* or an oil tanker of several hundred thousand tons.

> The only quality necessary to make a hero these days is boundless cheek, with a little foolhardiness thrown in. Any blackguard can sit in an aeroplane, and drop anything he wants.
>
> (*Cape Farewell*)

I would like the sea to be a source of moral inspiration and a way of finding meaning in, and guiding principles for, life on land. In my opinion, there is much that is useful and valuable to be acquired from our relationship with the sea, at least in a small craft. Humility, tenacity, patience, co-operation and respect. But above all, freedom. That is a paradox, of course. We are prisoners as nowhere else in a boat on the water. We can't leave it, can't do anything other than continue sailing if we want to survive. But at the same time we are freer than anywhere on land. Surrounded by an unbroken horizon, we are freer to dream of all potential or impossible lives ashore, free even to dream that life on land, for ourselves and for others, could be as good as it is when we have time to ourselves on a well-equipped vessel with no particular destination.

> The world must first be renewed, and this wonderful redeeming newness must be coaxed forth from people's souls. Until then there can only be broken relationships between broken fragments.
>
> (*Cape Farewell*)

On forging or severing bonds

'Isn't it dangerous living on board a boat?'

'Dangerous in what respect?'

'For your relationship.'

This brief exchange took place with someone to whom I had mentioned that Helle and I were living on board *Rustica* all year round, night and day, rain or shine.

I encountered similar reactions from others, some of whom vouchsafed their unsolicited and immutable opinions that they could never, at least not without going crazy, live in such close proximity to another person – and certainly not their spouse – as is unavoidable if you live on a small yacht.

Why then, one might ask with some justification, don't more people move in together on a boat for a trial period? They would soon find out whether there was any point in getting spliced.

It certainly seems to be true that life on board a sailing yacht reveals any defects or limitations in friendships and love relationships, as well as the converse. Sailing together either forges or severs bonds. Quite frankly, there is no middle way.

Many are the tales of good friends who on their arrival in the Canaries or the Caribbean put their boat on the market and went their separate ways. There are countless stories of married couples splitting up, acquaintances falling out. I myself knew two men who were sailing to the Mediterranean together: they ended up actually coming to blows.

If this is so, devotees of order and harmony will wonder whether it is worth the risk. Only the individuals concerned can answer that question. For me the answer is self-evident: what kind of friendship or love is it that can't stand proximity or silence?

~

When Sten and I had rounded the northernmost point of Denmark at Skagen after sailing the 480 nautical miles across the North Sea from Buckie in Scotland, it felt as if the voyage was over. The fact that we had to sail *Moana* right down to Kalvehave on southern Sjælland to complete our journey seemed a mere formality. Yet it was probably the hardest part of all beating down through the Great Belt pitching in rough seas. Wasn't it there that the forward hatch opened and let in considerable quantities of water? Wasn't it there that we were at our angriest and most depressed about the ghastly conditions? Wasn't it there that at dawn, after two wet tacks of five nautical miles each, I discovered that because of the current we had only made three nautical miles headway? Wasn't it there that the wind blew thirty-five miles an hour instead of the twenty-five that had been forecast?

Rational thinking is not necessarily characteristic of sailors. In the North Sea, bad weather filled us with dread and therefore inspired respect and caution. Here, where the threat to life and limb was minimal, we indulged in cursing and swearing at being 'at the mercy of the elements', as the expression has it. Not that curses would help. As if we would arrive any sooner in the little fishing port of Dybvig on Femø, where Sten's mother, grandmother and grandfather had sailed in his old fishing boat for the annual gathering of wooden boats.

But on we had to go and on we went, much to the delight of Sten especially. This was a fitting way of returning, we thought, instead of sailing direct to *Moana*'s home port to leave her there till the following spring. Because now with all the anxiety and trepidation of the North Sea crossings behind us, we didn't really want the voyage to end. Since Skagen we hadn't done much but wallow in our new-found nostalgia. At sea and in port between Aalbæk and Dybvig, a stretch of nearly two hundred nautical miles, we did nothing but talk of Scotland, of the waters and people we had met, not to speak of the whiskies we had sampled. We recapitulated everything, in the minutest detail, probably out of fear of forgetting.

I assume, without knowing for certain, that Sten, who was then no more than twenty-one, also felt a great sense of pride when we tied up in the modest harbour at Dybvig, absolutely full of wooden boats from the former fishing ports of Småland. A marquee had been erected for the festivities of the working boats' association, and that was where we found half of Sten's family ensconced.

But if I had expected our arrival to cause a certain commotion, I was wrong. Sten, inured by previous experience, was probably more realistic. His mother's relief at seeing her only son back in one piece was unmistakable, as was his grandmother's delight, but beyond that the interest in our return was nil. His uncle and grandfather, one an inveterate sailor, the other a fisherman by profession, asked not a single question about how it had been, showed not a sign of recognising anything remarkable in the fact that Sten, at such a youthful age, had sailed 1,600 nautical miles, of which 700 consisted of a double crossing of the North Sea, in a fairly spartan IF-boat. His uncle even began talking about the sky-high waves and terrible winds he had suffered during his own summer sailing in the Kattegat.

This, I couldn't help thinking, was a superb example of the 'Jante Law' of the Norwegian novelist Aksel Sandemose: 'Thou shalt not believe thou art something'. I was convinced for a long time that Sandemose had based his novel on his experience of the Danish island of Møn, south of Sjælland, but unfortunately it was the island of Mors in the Limfjord that he had in mind. 'Unfortunately', because it demonstrates that the validity of his 'Jante Law', commandments inspired by envy and parochialism, is depressingly widespread.

I asked Sten some time afterwards whether he had been questioned later about what it had been like. But no. None of his family or friends seemed the slightest bit inclined to hear about his experiences.

That, it seemed to me, was deeply unjust to Sten, even though he himself seemed to accept it. He still had his own memories, after all, as did I. And we had been bonded by the experience.

That same day in the marquee in Dybvig his grandmother, unprompted, asked me, 'How often did you quarrel?'

Sten was actually known as a temperamental character at home. But we didn't quarrel once during the entire voyage. When we were angry or surly we took it out on ourselves, not on each other.

That is one of the reasons why life on board ship can either forge a permanent bond or sever it completely. On long trips you have to choose to respect and consider others or else risk friendships ending for good. There isn't really any happy medium; keeping your head down and pretending nothing has happened isn't an option. Hypocrisy will inevitably be exposed and can only lead to one course: undermining and possibly sacrificing the relationship.

~

Janne Robertsson was my guest and part-time skipper on the *Moana* when we sailed to France. We were together nearly twenty-four hours a day for two months. We had our contentious discussions about architecture and concrete, and about choice of route from time to time, but that was all.

I rang Janne from Ireland a few years later and asked him if he would like to spend ten days sailing along the southern coast. He replied in the affirmative and turned up with his kitbag one evening in Crosshaven. He unpacked in less than a quarter of an hour and then we sat talking over a whisky and a cup of coffee till late. I think the feeling of continuing where we had left off was established within half an hour.

We set out the next morning in a heat haze and a fresh easterly. We handled the boat with barely a word exchanged. We had got the knack of working together down to a fine art.

It is satisfying to know a bond is so complete that you don't have to worry about how things will go. But perhaps the strangest thing of all is that a well-bonded crew never needs to be consciously considerate of one another. It's already in the alloy and the joints. Without that mutual care and consideration the joint would have come apart even before it had bonded.

One important rider has to be added to this: it is far from certain that the affinity engendered and strengthened at sea will function ashore. Any more than a friendship on land necessarily means you can sail together. Life at sea is a different kind of existence. Long-distance sailors in particular are known to be obstinate eccentrics. Why have sailors and fishermen always found it so hard to adjust to life ashore?

'*There is no reliable guide to manners for a seafarer,*' Harry Martinson writes in *Aimless Travels*. '*Nor can it be taken for granted that he loves his country, i.e. that element of him where his own manners should by law and custom be rooted.*

Many people think of the pirates of old as criminals fleeing retribution on land. That is a misconception. Pirates were seamen first and criminals second. They didn't want thieves and murderers on board. Pirates maintained – with good reason, we have to assume – that it was much easier to make pirates of (honest) sailors than to turn criminals into sailors.

Then of course we may wonder what it is that persuades some to go to sea and not others. That might provide a good topic for research. But as so often where human beings are concerned the answer will almost certainly be too complex to lend itself to much more than hypotheses and qualified guesses.

One may make assumptions about facts and winds. One may guess how many blades of grass there are under an upturned tub, and how many mussels in one bay or another.

But to guess anything about human beings is sheer folly. They are deceptive.

(*Aimless Travels*)

Quite right.

On two anchorages in the Outer Hebrides

Helle and I put out from Tobermory on Mull to make our first voyage round Ardnamurchan Point, beyond which they say real sailing begins. When you meet yachts in southern Scotland with a sprig of heather on the pulpit, you know they have been 'north of Ardnamurchan'. They have sailed where you have to rely entirely on your own judgement and take total responsibility for your actions. From Ardnamurchan Point up to Cape Wrath there isn't a single marina or even protective mole to give shelter from winds and waves. You sail very much at your own risk.

We had listened to several consecutive weather forecasts and decided that this was a suitable day to expose ourselves to the Atlantic swells. Others had had the same thought, that now was the moment to try for the isolated islands before the next depression came racing in over Scotland from the Atlantic.

An old couple in Tobermory had advised us that the best way of determining whether it was possible to round Ardnamurchan was to observe the breakers on New Rocks. If the swell was breaking there, you might as well turn your prow in the opposite direction.

There was no trace of surf that day. When the Atlantic opened out before us we were looking straight into a thick, milky bank of mist resembling mother-of-pearl in the strong sunlight from the east. Yet the mist seemed to be receding steadily ahead of us as we advanced. To starboard lay Rhum, the largest and most majestic of what are called The Small Isles, a name they only merit because they are smaller than Mull and Skye. They can hardly be called small in themselves. When we sighted Rhum's 2,500-foot mountain from a distance, we naturally enough thought it was Skye, not one of the so-called 'small' islands marked on the chart. We searched the sea in vain for several low islands until it occurred to us that we had misread the chart simply because of a name. So we learnt the banal but essential lesson that some yardstick is needed to assess little and large. Despite our earlier visits, we had still not got the measure of Scotland or comprehended its vast dimensions. We always had the flat islands of Denmark and the low convex skerries of Sweden's west coast of Bohuslän in the back of our minds.

We sailed all morning past the bare, rust-coloured mountainside of Rhum while the sun evaporated the last of the mist. It was here that we saw our first whale sporting in the currents between the islands.

At about two o'clock the sound between Canna and Rhum appeared before us, just as the light wind died altogether. There was a strong adverse current running between the islands and we did the last bit under power. At three o'clock we glided slowly into the smooth lagoon between the islands of Canna and Sanday. All was peaceful and quiet. There was one boat there before us. Later that evening two more turned up, and by the time dusk fell we were five, and none of us disturbed the reverent serenity.

We went ashore soon after arriving. We began by climbing to the highest point on Canna, from which we had an uninterrupted view in all directions. To the north towered the sheer three-thousand-foot mountain of Skye. To the west, thirty-five nautical miles away, we could see the silhouette of the southernmost islands of the Outer Hebrides: Barra, South and North Uist. To the southwest there was nothing but open sea. Mull was visible to the southeast, and beyond it the snow-covered summit of Ben Nevis. Closest to us in the east the distinctively-coloured contours of Rhum looked like an irregular Egyptian pyramid. Beyond it lay the Scottish mainland with billowy white cumulus clouds over the peaks. At our feet were the calm waters of the natural harbour between Canna and Sanday, the two islands that popularly go under the single name of Canna.

Evening descended on us solemnly in the still air of the northern sunset. We sat on board *Rustica* with a whisky chatting to Gordon about Scotland and Canna.

Canna is one of many forgotten islands in the Hebrides. There is no regular boat connection from the mainland. The handful of families living on Canna and Sanday have to get by as best they may. The owner of the island for over forty years, John Lorne Campbell, has devoted much of his life to fighting for himself and the other islanders to continue living there, but has mostly met with indifference and incomprehension. The authorities in Oban and Glasgow must wonder why anyone would want to live on an island like Canna. If Campbell and the other inhabitants had not taken matters into their own hands, if they had just tried to get by with occasional practical or financial support, their battle would already have been lost. But they have built themselves a jetty to enable them to ferry cattle off the island for slaughter, they have maintained the only road on the island themselves and repaired the footbridge between Canna and Sanday several times after heavy winter storms. They have done what they could to enable themselves to live remote from the modern world, with its queues of cars, its supermarkets, fashion boutiques, restaurants, daily papers, crèches, petrol stations, libraries and cinemas. There are people like them in most coastal areas, people who never give up the struggle to be able to stay where they are.

Gordon lived just outside Glasgow, where he worked part-time as a fireman. He devoted his free time to his greatest passion in life: Scotland. Despite not having much money he paid about ten pounds a month to the National Trust to help preserve and maintain Scotland's ancient monuments. He asked whether we had visited the old church at the eastern end of Sanday, and it was obvious how saddened he was by its state of decay.

We met many like Gordon on our travels around Scotland. 'Ordinary' people who spoke about their country in a way that I had never encountered in Sweden or France. It may simply be the capriciousness of chance, but I have never met anyone from Skåne in southern Sweden who was personally bothered by the fact that only holidaymakers now inhabit the sparsely populated regions of northern Sweden, the outer skerries of Stockholm or the forests of Värmland.

Though sometimes I am inclined to believe that the Scots' love of Scotland has more to do with the country than with the people. In his book *Hebridean Connection*, Derek Cooper writes, 'I know few places in the world which have such an ability to improve on nature as the Hebrides. It has something to do with ultra violet rays, I'm told, but the intensity of the light, its magical powers of magnification and its aggrandisement of colour are to me unparalleled elsewhere.'

～

When we woke next day a mist had settled over Canna and Sanday. The big islands, Skye and Mull, had vanished as if they had never existed, and so had the small ones, Rhum, Eigg and Muck. We went for a walk over the rocks on Sanday. We had only intended going round the island by the shore (as if we hadn't had enough of the sea; but that's how it is, our walks nearly always end up at the water's edge). But we had to turn back. When we climbed a slope and reached the top we came face to face with a herd of Highland cattle stepping out of the mist like primeval aurochs with their curved pointed horns and shaggy hair. We tried to convince ourselves that these were just cows like any others. But in vain. They still looked like dangerous prehistoric monsters. We beat a hasty retreat and went back the way we had come, with one more memory of Scotland and the Hebrides to add to our collection.

～

The following day when we woke the mist had been dispersed by a fresh southerly breeze. The sun was shining bright and clear. Fluffy cumulus clouds were drifting past above our heads. We weighed anchor with some difficulty because of the seaweed and set off towards the Outer Hebrides, our proposed adventure for this trip.

Aided by the Clyde Cruising Club's descriptions we had selected Loch-skipport on South Uist as our first port of call. It was relatively simple to identify and enter. There was an abundance of safe protected anchorages to choose from within the sea loch.

In the crystal-clear air we sighted Mount Hecla, due south of Loch-skipport, as soon as we were a few nautical miles out of Canna. All we had to do was steer straight ahead with a steady wind on beam reach that gave us a good speed. We had our Decca yacht navigator now, but all the pilot books warned against relying on it in the Outer Hebrides.

At about five o'clock, with a few nautical miles still to go, our Decca not unexpectedly began to show signs of uncertainty. But by then we had already identified the entrance channel among the myriad rocks covered in nothing but moss, heather and ferns. Not a tree in sight. The only colours were the gneiss-grey of the rocks, the deep blue of sea and sky and the bright green of the windswept undergrowth. But that was more than enough.

The wind slackened as we neared land. On the way in to Lochskip-port itself we had a fresh headwind, probably because of Mount Hecla, which is notorious among those familiar with it for its violent katabatic winds in strong westerlies. At half past five in the afternoon we laid the anchor chain through the hawse in an almost totally enclosed pool, as big as two football pitches, but circular, called Cadan Mor. We were alone apart from some seals which turned up as soon as we had cut the engine. They swam round the boat regarding us inquisitively.

When we rowed ashore in the tender they followed us, four seal heads one behind the other. We climbed a hill and saw the open Atlantic spread out to the west. The mighty bulk of Skye rose in the north-east. The air, as always when the sun was out, was as clear as new-blown glass.

The wind dropped again during the evening. The only sounds were the snuffling and splashing of the seals, an anxious mother gull squawking and some cawing crows on land. That was all. The tranquillity was complete. The world beyond Cadan Mor might not have existed.

We lay up in Cadan Mor until our bread ran out. We saw two other boats at anchor in similar pools in Lochskipport while we were there. A fisherman came by in an open boat with an outboard motor to check his nets. That was all as far as men and machines were concerned. Yet this was around midsummer's day, the beginning of the sailing season in these parts.

~

When we set off for Scotland the second time it had been our fervent wish to get to the Outer Hebrides. I can quite see that people might wonder why. What is the point of sailing out to some bare, barren and chilly islands that are rightly renowned, not to say infamous, for their atrocious weather?

The answer must lie in dreams: the dream of experiencing something incomparable, something that will leave an indelible impression on soul and heart, something that can never be conveyed in books or films, on TV or CD-ROM. Not virtual reality, as apparent three dimensions are now called in computer jargon, but actual reality, undistorted by man's inability to leave well alone, and in many more dimensions than a paltry three.

But the dream of such experiences is not that easy to realise, not even in a sailing yacht. When you least expect it some pot-bellied man will turn up in an equally pot-bellied luxury cruiser, with or without sail, that you know must have cost a few hundred thousand and gets used a couple of weeks a year. Or some stout helmsman will be yelling orders at his nervous wife who is having to push out a boat weighing several tons. Not to mention half a dozen middle-aged men drinking themselves paralytic with raucous shouting and joyless outbursts of laughter. And so the mood of the day is destroyed.

If you want to associate with people in reasonable human doses and also experience beauty and peace, there are not many places left to choose from except those that have a bad reputation for weather or wind.

In the Outer Hebrides there are thousands of such anchorages, all equally as desolate as Lochskipport. You could sail a whole lifetime of summers among these islands without seeing everything or becoming sated.

Obviously there can be weeks when the rain pours down from an overcast grey sky and gale-force winds batter the ears. There can be days when you yearn for warmer and more immediately hospitable waters, perhaps even for sandy beaches, street cafés and night-life in a T-shirt.

But then the skies clear and you ask yourself in astonishment if you were in your right mind to want to be anywhere other than the Hebrides. Luckily most people answer that question in the affirmative. So luckily northern Scotland will continue for the foreseeable future to be just as bleak, windy, rainy and cold as it always has been. And luckily natural harbours such as Canna and Lochskipport will always suffer a magnificent dearth of maritime civilisation.

You would light a cigarette and think. You were so powerful and so small that you could almost weep.

(Cape Farewell)

On drinking customs

One evening like many a similar one I was sitting in our local pub, the Tap Tavern in Kinsale. Next to me sat two elderly men drinking what looked like Guinness, the dark, velvety and bitter national drink of Ireland. Nothing unusual in that. Except that the two men were drinking their Guinness in half-pint glasses, instead of pint mugs. I had heard that it was only women who drank Guinness in halves; (real) men always ordered pints.

So I turned to one of them and asked what they were doing drinking Guinness in halves. As a foreigner and guest in their country, I said, I wanted to know how to do things properly, and I'd heard that the only way to drink Guinness was in pints.

Broad grins spread over their faces. One of them leant forward, winked knowingly and confided, "Tis not Guinness. 'Tis Murphy's.'

It was as simple as that. Murphy's is the closest rival to the national emblem of Guinness. You could take liberties with Murphy's. But not with Guinness.

~

Another evening I was at the little bar in Peter and Barbara's restaurant. They were English and had lived in Kinsale for nearly eight years. Not that they had intended to. Barbara was just passing through with a girl friend. Peter was taken to Ireland by a friend and happened to end up in Kinsale.

The two found each other there, opened a restaurant, and often said that it was high time they moved on. But still they stay.

'Kinsale is lethal,' said Peter, who knew what he was talking about, since he'd travelled half the world. 'It's lethal for the wallet and for the health. It's altogether too enjoyable here.'

Kinsale *is* enjoyable, and particularly in winter when people have time to be convivial and chat to their guests and each other. Kinsale must have one of the highest concentrations of pubs and restaurants in the world.

As we stood there talking, in came John on his way home. It wasn't difficult to see that he'd had one too many, even by Irish standards. He was well and truly inebriated. But not unpleasant with it or noisy or quarrelsome. Though I did find it hard to understand what he was saying.

Barbara introduced me, and it wasn't long, only a matter of seconds in fact, before John offered me a drink. Having intended going back to *Rustica* to work, in other words to write, I politely declined. John, who could not in his wildest fantasies have envisaged a negative answer, was already ordering two glasses. I was about to repeat my refusal when Barbara gestured to me to accept his offer.

When he had left, Barbara apologised for having led me into temptation. 'But John would have taken it very badly if you had refused pointblank to drink with him. Refusing generosity and hospitality is one of the worst crimes you can commit in this country.'

~

I arrived in Crosshaven just south of Cork in August, after having sailed solo the two hundred nautical miles from Dublin. From that trip I remember in particular the stretch from Arklow to Dunmore East and meeting the Atlantic. I set sail at five in the morning, partly in order to be able to make the seventy nautical miles in a day, and partly to be sure of having the tide with me when I rounded Tuskar Rock, the last outpost of southeast Ireland where the current can run at five to six knots. There wasn't much wind, so I motored. Tuskar Rock lighthouse appeared over the horizon at about the same time as I felt the current begin to push *Rustica* from behind. Faster and faster we went. But then the tidal current met a counter-swell from the Atlantic that I hadn't reckoned on at all. The waves got bigger and bigger and yet for some incomprehensible reason levelled out, as if oil had been poured on the water. When we passed Tuskar Rock and I saw the open Atlantic before me, the waves were about four metres high. Without a breath of wind!

I freely admit that this gave me pause for thought, in my present single-handed situation. What would it be like here in a gale and with the wind against the current? It would be an inferno, no more nor less. With the current from the stern there would be nowhere else to go, either. It was simply impossible to turn back. My stomach lurched when we plunged down one of the gigantic waves.

But I got round the south-east corner of Ireland with great velocity and sailed into Dunmore East an hour or so before the fog descended like a thick soup. And I thanked my lucky stars that all had gone well. What would I have done if the fog had arrived earlier? Sailed on to Cork and tried an approach in the middle of the night? Hove to and waited till the fog cleared, increasingly uncertain of my position? Sailing, especially single-handed, and especially along the Atlantic coast of Ireland, is far from being a gentle comfort for the soul.

I reached Crosshaven without a hitch, anyway. I was intending to stay there a week and wait for Janne Robertsson, who was going to come with me on an inshore cruise from Cork to the Fastnet Rock.

I rarely suffer from loneliness. Solitude gives me an incomparable feeling of freedom. Fundamentally I think it is loneliness, the price to be paid for total freedom, which makes so few people able to live an entirely unfettered life. For myself it takes a long time before loneliness outweighs my feeling of freedom. When I was younger, not so self-assured and shyer with strangers, I spent three months in Paris more or less without speaking to anyone. Without suffering unduly and without being lonely.

Nowadays I don't have such fortitude and do seek out a bit of human company.

In Crosshaven I used the same method I had employed successfully when I moved to Paris and to Copenhagen without knowing a soul. I started by trying all the pubs, cafés and bars I came across. I would buy a drink, observe the customers, absorb the atmosphere, and decide on a place to make my local for the duration.

As in most Irish towns with any self-respect, and that seems to be the vast majority, Crosshaven had no lack of licensed premises. The entire har-bourfront was replete with hand-painted pub signs.

I decided eventually on a pub called Bucklie's. On my very first visit the proprietress, a blonde in what seemed to be her prime (about fifty), asked me my name, where I came from, what I was doing in Crosshaven and my impressions of Ireland. There wasn't the slightest hint of distrust in her questions, just human curiosity. Everywhere in Ireland and Scotland people asked your name, a legacy, I suspect, from the Celts. To forget a person's name, for the Celts, was equivalent to killing him.

The next day she introduced me to several regulars with whom I exchanged a few words about my sailing. By the third day I was as good as a regular myself and was greeted by name as soon as I came in the door.

This was not by any means unique to Bucklie's in Crosshaven. We had the same experiences all over Ireland.

I usually measure a country's hospitality by its citizens' readiness to accept foreigners and make them feel at home. In that respect we have an incredible amount to learn and as much to be ashamed of in Sweden – and so by the way do France, Spain and Denmark, countries which have no dearth of public life and café or pub culture. In Spain people seem so involved with their own circles, usually the whole extended family, that they have no time to socialise with outsiders. In France, café life is fairly private or something for weary semi-alcoholics. There, it is restaurants where ordinary people gather, but restaurants aren't really the place to be interested in the welfare of your neighbours. And in Denmark it can take months before you're allowed into the warmth.

Another way of measuring the psychological health of a country would be to check their attitude to beer, wine and spirits. Any comparison by that criterion would look bad for Sweden. In other countries with which I am acquainted people may be drunk when they go home. Or they go home when they start to notice they are drunk. In all my years in France I have never, ever, met anyone who was drunk, sloshed, pissed, or whatever term you prefer. In Sweden the opposite seems to apply: people drink themselves into a state of inebriation before they go out. Or in order to give themselves the courage to go out. In Sweden we laugh conspiratorially at people who boast of how much they have been able to pour down their throats or knock back in an evening and still somehow or other be able to stagger home, with vomit stuck to the soles of their shoes. In Sweden we find it amusing to hear the story of how few people would venture to invite the author Fritiof Nilsson Piraten to their house because if rumours were to be believed (and maybe they were no more than rumours), he would never go home until all the bottles of spirit were empty.

If you read French package holiday brochures you'll find here and there a little phrase under the heading 'full board': '*Vin à discrétion*'. For a Swede that must be something unheard of, akin to paradise. *Vin à discrétion* means that unlimited quantities of wine are included in the price. But what does the word *discrétion* actually mean in this context? It means you can drink as much as you like, but judiciously, that is to say without shaming yourself! For all too many Swedes it would be synonymous with being able to drink any amount.

It is hard to find adequate invective for this Swedish phenomenon, which turns drunkenness, vomiting, memory loss, yelling and screaming, slurred speech and stumbling into a test of virility, something to go around boasting about – even though there's nothing easier than getting drunk and behaving badly. As far as attitude to beer, wine and spirits is concerned, Sweden – with very few exceptions – has not matured beyond puberty.

I sat one evening in Bucklie's in conversation with an electrician called John. He said he had only been abroad once, and that was to Crosshaven's twin town in Brittany. That one occasion had given him memories to last for the rest of his life. He had arrived a few hours in advance of all the others, which had led the French to believe that he was the mayor of Crosshaven. So he had received a regal reception in the town hall, with handshakes and champagne, all the while wondering desperately what was going on. He wasn't able to ask because he didn't know a word of French!

As we sat there chatting John bought me a beer. When a little later on I wanted to return the compliment, he said quietly, 'No, you can do that tomorrow. I was buying today. I wasn't intending us to be drinking together.'

And so I learnt another lesson.

He had sailed here on sublime waves, over unsullied oceans – to drink spirits as usual.

I led him on board. He followed me like a calf stupefied by the heat.

Where was the divine spark? Not in his dulled brain, anyway. He stumbled on the quay, his knees buckled, and he fell against me and said, 'Anders, Bahia is a bloody awful town, every town is a bloody awful town.'

(*Aimless Travels*)

On being in a small boat on the wide open sea

When Helle woke up at about five in the morning we had not much more than eighty nautical miles left to Fraserburgh. During my night watch we had sailed through a supernatural landscape of oil-rigs, illuminated like Christmas trees. You get a strange feeling at the thought of several thousand people living and working right out in the sea. It was as if we were sailing through a city.

And yet a completely inaccessible one. The platforms stand thirty metres above the water, and even if we were allowed to – there is a safety exclusion zone of five hundred metres around them – it would be impossible to tie up, stop for a while and have a conversation. Out in the North Sea we on *Rustica* and the people on the rigs inhabit two utterly different worlds: one of high technology, suspended between heaven and earth, with videos and helicopters, welding gear and restaurants, apartments and table-tennis tables, with work schedules and confinement – the other, our world, exposed to the elements, magnificent and capricious, uplifting or frightening, refreshing or exhausting, a world in constant flux where nothing can ever be taken for granted.

When dawn broke the platforms had vanished from sight. The sun rose in a cloudless sky. The sea was only lightly ruffled. Eighty nautical miles to go, and 260 behind us. If it holds, we thought, we can count ourselves lucky. The wind had been just right, no mist to speak of, not much rain, no thunderstorms; we had so far escaped all the factors that can turn a sea cruise into an excruciatingly hazardous venture.

At ten to six Helle picked up the weather forecast from the BBC. It came as quite a shock on that calm sunny sea. Gale warning, force eight, forty-five miles an hour, from the south-east. We gazed at one another in disbelief. How could it be possible? The sea couldn't have looked more inviting, almost as if polished smooth, hardly any swell, not the slightest hint of approaching storms.

'Did they give any time?' I asked.

'No.'

Which meant we ought to have twelve hours' grace before it hit us. That was something, but it wasn't enough to get us into harbour. We couldn't hope to do more than five and a half knots. We counted up. We would have at best ten nautical miles still to go by the time it really set in. And it would be dark, the tide would be against us and we would be sailing in shallow waters and approaching Rattray Head in seas renowned for their difficulty in strong winds. Two lifeboats had capsized with total loss of crew in those very shipping lanes off Rattray Head. It said so in our pilot book. Would we even be able to put in to Fraserburgh when we arrived? And we would be on a down wind. It was hard to imagine any worse prospect, apart from even fiercer winds.

How many sailors must have asked themselves as we did what was the best action to take on hearing a gale warning? How many must have felt their hearts flutter in the certain knowledge that everything would look so different in a few hours' time? How many must have sat weighing up the imponderables: how long would the gale last, what would the wind direction be, would the wind increase, what was the state of the sea in the harbour entrance? How many must have entertained a ray of hope that the meteorological office had made a mistake and lived up to all the jokes about their staff outings in pouring rain? But no, the only thing that is virtually certain is that weather forecasts are seldom wrong. The strength and direction of the wind can vary slightly, it can reach its peak earlier or later, but the bad weather nearly always comes as forecast.

So we sat there in our little boat feeling rather vulnerable. What choices did we have? To heave to or keep going, to reef the sails and ride out the storm, or to sail on.

This time we kept going. We motored at full speed all morning on the completely calm smooth water. Not until midday did the wind start getting up enough to rouse the sea to anything that merited being called waves. We made two reefs in the mainsail and one in the jib. We stowed everything away or lashed it down. The weather forecast from the BBC at one o'clock put an end to any vestige of hope. And this time they added the word 'imminent'. So we could reckon on the gale being over us within six hours.

The wind gradually increased all afternoon. The waves slowly and inexorably rose. It was blowing from the south-east and gave us a down wind, exactly like the time before in *Moana* when it also blew up from the stern in the last few hours on our way into Fraserburgh. But we could already see that this was going to be worse.

The autopilot was still managing to steer, despite the down wind. (The uninitiated will need to know that a down wind means it is coming straight in over the stern, bringing a risk of gybing if you are not careful. Gybing means that the wind blows into the back of the mainsail, which with a down wind is at a right angle to the wind direction, and can swing the sail to the opposite side with immense force, so powerfully in fact that in the worst case it can snap the mast.)

But the autopilot was having to work harder and harder to keep us on course. In the most violent gusts we began rather alarmingly to point higher to the wind (once again some seamanship tuition for landlubbers: to point higher means that the wind comes more from the front than before). In our case, with a long-keeled boat like *Rustica*, it transformed our relatively moderate and steady speed into a mighty surge forward, spray flying, the boat heeling further over and a much greater strain on the sail.

At about the same time as the autopilot started having problems I discovered to my horror that the fifteen-kilo bow anchor had shaken itself loose. The pin in the stem mounting had fallen out and now it looked as if the anchor was on its way over the rail. In my mind's eye I could see the pointed fluke smashing a huge hole in the freeboard.

It is precisely in situations like this that mistakes can be made. To avoid one danger you can so easily and unthinkingly expose yourself to another when under pressure. This time I had enough presence of mind to attach my lifeline to the wire running along the deck from bow to stern. But I might easily have rushed forward, head over heels, without considering my own safety. Which would have been worse? A hole in the side or an oblique wave knocking me overboard? The latter, I suppose.

I released the anchor from its chain, with some difficulty because the shackle was fastened with steel wire, and carried it astern, bent double. I opened the locker in the cockpit and stowed the anchor among the sailbags. Then it was high time to take over from the autopilot for good. In the stronger gusts *Rustica* had begun to point higher so that we were almost sailing on close reach, and were racing ahead like a bolting horse before the autopilot could react. And when it did, it over-reacted. The turn of the rudder was too great, so we came dangerously close to a gybe on the course that was meant to compensate for our veering into the wind.

This, by the way, was a supreme and instructive example of the limitations of technology. Modern autopilots are sophisticated machines full of electronics and microchips. They are even able to learn, with the memories of elephants. They take account of the waves, or more precisely of the boat's behaviour in the water. The autopilot stores information on deviations from course, ignoring any 'false alarms', that is those which do not actually throw the boat off course.

So why are they unable to compete with human helmsmen? Well, it is not strength. There are autopilots that can develop 75 kiloponds. Nor exhaustion. An autopilot does not need to eat and sleep, as long as it has enough electricity. So what can't it do? Two things: it cannot foresee what is going to happen and it cannot make exceptions to the rule.

A human helmsman has the wonderful advantage of being able to see ahead, or for that matter astern, and can begin to compensate for a huge wave before it has crashed over the boat. And the autopilot can only learn from regular occurrences. It sticks to principles, so to speak. Human beings possess the extremely valuable yet mysterious ability to identify a wave that does not look like any other, to judge something as being an exception to any rule. It is this factor, of course, which has been one of the main obstacles to the creation of artificial intelligence. Computers have to work according to rules, whereas human beings can work according to individual cases as well as to rules, without going insane.

Nowhere do we have greater need for that ability than when sitting at the helm steering through a boiling chaos of irregular waves, where every single wave is an exception to any rule.

It was eight o'clock when I took over from the autopilot for the rest of the evening and night. At the same time we shut the hatch and Helle sat down at the chart table to navigate us into port with the aid of the Decca. We were pleased we had changed the wooden washboards for centimetre-thick plexiglass and the sliding hatch for a skylight. Partly because we knew the entrance was watertight, partly, and perhaps most importantly, because we could keep eye contact through the plexiglass. It would have been no fun for Helle and me to be sitting in two separate worlds in the hours to come. Just being able to check the waves astern before opening the hatch to say a few words or to give me a cigarette was worth a great deal.

Not that we had very much to talk about. We each had our job to do. My eyes were moving continuously between the compass and the threads on the shrouds that indicated from which direction the wind was striking the sail at any given instant. My task was simple: to make sure we didn't make an accidental gybe.

But the situation was complicated by several factors. Firstly, as all sailors know, the wind didn't keep blowing consistently from the same direction. What at one moment can be a safe course within margins can quickly change to a course with a risk of gybing on the next gust of wind if you don't compensate with the rudder. Secondly, we were on the port tack, which meant that the mainsail was pointing out to starboard. That in turn meant that I had to be extremely careful not to steer more than necessary to starboard if there were the threat of a gybe. No problem to port as far as a gybe was concerned. Except that land lay on the port side, and we needed all the sea room we could get.

So it was obvious I had to keep on full alert. In order not to get too close to shore I had to steer the boat to starboard as much as I dared, but not so much as to risk a gybe. Balancing this knife-edge course was all the more essential because in a few hours' time the tidal current would turn southwards and push us relentlessly inshore.

As if that weren't enough, we also had to allow for the fact that we were approaching shallower waters, which always make the sea choppier. The charts and the pilot books warn of sandbanks off Rattray Head thus: 'breaks heavily in rough seas'. It was Helle's responsibility to make sure that I didn't steer us right over these shallows. She put her head out from time to time and gave me a new course. The worst was when she advised a few degrees to starboard, if I could risk it.

What with the shore, gybing, tide and shallows, there was plenty to think about, but on top of that it was getting dark and the sky looked as if it might open at any moment and release the Flood...

∼

By about nine in the evening the waves were becoming huge, and some were breaking with a great roar. On the other hand, the wind didn't feel so strong because we had it behind us and were making six or seven knots when we plunged down to the bottom of a trough. We never made this speed ourselves: it was the waves moving faster than us (the opposite, the boat sailing faster than the waves, is especially dangerous, since you can drive your bows at full tilt into the wave ahead and be brought up sharp before being caught by the next wave from behind and flipped over). At the bottom of the troughs there was almost no wind at all for a brief instant before the next wave lifted us up towards the blue-grey sky.

The wind was still increasing.

I asked Helle to contact the coastguard in Aberdeen on the VHF radio.

She might be able to get some advice on how the weather would develop, for instance when we could expect the wind to reach its maximum. It felt unreal to see her sitting there talking on the telephone behind the plexiglass.

She popped her head out afterwards looking somewhat disconsolate to say that they couldn't give an opinion. But they said that we should keep at least five nautical miles offshore, that there was no question of putting into Fraserburgh and that we should keep them informed of our progress and when we eventually got into harbour.

Later, when we were safely in harbour, Helle told me the whole story. The coastguard had also asked how many we were on board. When Helle replied 'Two' she got a spontaneous and very British 'Oh'. You could imagine that an American in the same position would have used a coarser expression like 'Oh shit!' It was hardly encouraging, but I was happily unaware of that in the cockpit under the steel-grey darkening skies trying to keep my eyes peeled.

It turned out, however, that my own experience proved useful. Sten and I had also had a south-easterly gale behind us, though not quite as fierce, when we were running into Fraserburgh in the *Moana* a few years before. On that occasion we were in the lee of Rattray Head and had been able to put into Fraserburgh as planned. Why not now? So Helle called up the harbourmaster in Fraserburgh, explained the situation and asked if he thought we could get in. To which came the good-natured reply, with rolling Scottish r's, 'No prrroblem, no prrroblem!'

But that opinion was about the harbour entrance, not about our passage, which was far from being 'no prrroblem'. To get to Fraserburgh at all we would have to come in closer to land and so into shallower water, and thus over the sandbanks for which the pilot books issued special warnings about breaking seas in strong onshore winds.

Whether it was because we came too close to the sandbanks after all, I am not sure, but I suddenly noticed that in the last feeble evening light *Rustica* was rising on a wave that was steeper and higher than any of the others we had so far encountered. And there was another after that, and another, the last, with cascading breaking crests. I managed to parry the first two by letting *Rustica* skim down with the wave on the quarter, meaning diagonally from behind. Nothing could help against the third, at least nothing within my competence as helmsman. The wave broke with a crash somewhere astern of us and sent a few hundred litres of water into the cockpit, most of it over and beside me and on the plexiglass of the companionway. When the water had run off I could see Helle's indistinct anxious features behind the streaming glass. I nodded to indicate that all was well. The fourth wave had already passed and was significantly smaller than the previous ones.

The danger was over for this time and we carried on as before, with Helle at the chart table and me at the tiller.

Afterwards I congratulated myself on another measure taken long beforehand, sealing in the engine instruments and ignition key behind a plexiglass cover with a rubber seal. They were positioned right under the companionway and were deluged with water from the breaking wave. It would have been no joke having to berth under sail if the engine wouldn't start when and if we came into harbour.

A moment later I caught a glimpse of something out of the corner of my eye. I admit I'd been a bit careless about keeping a lookout for other vessels. Partly, I reasoned to myself, because there were no large commercial ports ahead, and partly because there couldn't be anyone who was crazy enough to put to sea in this weather.

But there was.

When I turned my head I saw to my amazement a massive deep-sea trawler coming towards us a few hundred yards to starboard. In the next second it was buried in wash and spray before it reappeared, ploughing ahead on its easterly course, straight out into the North Sea, straight into fifteen- to twenty-foot waves. Three thoughts struck me: firstly, horror-stricken relief that we had not been on a collision course; would I – or the trawler – have been able to veer away? Secondly, disbelief: here were we in *Rustica* wanting nothing but to be in port, while the trawler crew were actually going out in this weather to work; for them this was a normal working day! Thirdly, they must know that the gale was not going to last long. Which was some consolation.

A few moments later the trawler was out of sight and we continued hurtling through the blackness of the night. At this stage Helle was drawing up positions and courses every ten minutes, both to know where we were and, I suspect, to avoid having to sit unoccupied in a hermetically sealed cabin.

Our distance from the shore was decreasing all the time, despite the Aberdeen coastguards' warning, even though we were waiting till we had Fraserburgh abeam before setting our prow straight towards harbour. I don't know how long we still had to go when I began to think that the sea was slightly calmer. But if I remember correctly we could already make out the lights ashore. In any event it was fairly insignificant right then. The important thing was that exactly as last time we had passed into the lee of Rattray Head and could in theory get into Fraserburgh harbour. I say 'in theory' partly because the waves were still very big, though they had lost their malevolent sting and the worst of their immense weight as they broke, and partly because we still had to find a forty-yard-wide gap behind thirty-foot-high breakwaters in the pitch dark.

In addition to that, the wind showed no signs of abating. Quite the opposite, in fact. We had about one and a half nautical miles to go. I'd been given a course by Helle which should take us straight into the harbour entrance. As we were now sailing on close reach we were flying ahead at seven or eight knots, despite our seven tons, long keel, double-reefed mainsail and single-reefed jib. It was then, with only twenty minutes left, that I felt a sudden freshening of the wind from one second to the next. I beckoned Helle to come out, explained the situation and that we would have to take down the mainsail. Not simply because we had too much sail up, but primarily because it had just occurred to me that we would have a stern wind again when we turned into harbour. In my imagination I could see *Rustica* scudding in at eight or nine knots with limited room for manoeuvre.

I could barely wait for Helle to grip the tiller before I made myself fast to the lifeline and clambered over the deck. At the same time I uttered words that were to become immortal on board *Rustica*: 'Steer straight ahead!'

When I came back after having got the mainsail down and somehow more or less furling it, Helle quite rightly asked how you steer straight ahead in a boat with no fixed point on land, in total darkness and without a set course on the compass.

I had no answer to that. But it was fortunate anyway that we got the mainsail down. We were still doing six knots on nothing but a reefed jib when we finally flew in between the high breakwaters. We switched on the engine, which thankfully started at once, only to discover that we couldn't use it to brake. *Rustica* has a variable-pitch propeller instead of reverse thrust, and the friction of the water against the propeller blades was so great that it was impossible to turn it in reverse. So we had to sail into the first harbour basin we came to and make several circuits with neither sail nor engine in order to slow down enough to be able to motor both backwards and forwards.

Should anyone think this all sounds exaggerated or unbelievable, we can compare our experience with the single-handed German sailor who came in two hours after us in a Monsoon. He told us the next morning that he had been making four knots from the rigging alone, without a single sail up. It was scarcely surprising that his first action the following morning was to crack open a bottle of champagne to celebrate still being alive. That was probably the one and only time I drank champagne for breakfast on an empty stomach. But it was also the day we learnt that the wind had gusted at gale force nine on the Beaufort scale, which is up to fifty-five miles an hour.

Only when the situation was pretty well under control did we have time to look around for a place to tie up. Imagine our surprise when we heard ourselves being hailed by a shadowy figure on the end of one of the jetties high above our heads. It was the harbourmaster waiting for us at two o'clock in the morning, perhaps because his 'no problem' on the VHF had been something of a British understatement after all, and he was accustomed to advising deep-sea trawlers rather than 35-foot yachts. He waved us into a basin where there was already one lone yacht bucking up and down at the quayside. But I knew it would be calmer further in and sailed into the next basin at a fair lick.

We found an English yacht in the inner basin to moor alongside. It was a sloppy approach on my part, at too high a speed, saved only by Helle and a member of the crew on the English boat. But by that stage I was past worrying about little things like scratches on the freeboard and dented pulpits. The moment we sailed in between Fraserburgh's enormous break-waters I became supremely carefree. We had saved *Rustica* and our own skins, and that was all that mattered.

Helle found it harder to get her adrenalin back down to a normal level. When we had tied up she absolutely had to have firm ground beneath her feet. She had to climb over a yacht, three fishing boats and up a 20-foot ladder to reach the jetty and recover from the worst of her excitement. I was quite content to stay sitting or standing where I was.

Below deck everything looked chaotic, with boots and oilskins all over the place. But it took only a few minutes to make the cabin ship-shape. We had stowed everything ready for the North Sea; even the cushions on the saloon berths had been tied down with the thin cords and hooks that we had sewn and screwed in for the purpose. Helle sat at the chart table one last time, called up the Aberdeen coastguards as promised and told them we were safely in harbour. We could detect a certain relief in the courteous British tones.

Finally we poured ourselves a generous malt whisky of a superior brand. The strange thing was that for once it tasted flat and flavourless. It seemed as if we couldn't take in any more sensations.

But what a delight it was to be sitting there at two o'clock in the morning in *Rustica*'s cabin, in Fraserburgh's enormous harbour, in Scot-land, on the other side of the North Sea, after a successfully completed passage, safely moored, with the wind howling in the rigging and with a decent if somewhat lacklustre whisky in our hands! There was no hurry for anything. All our problems were over. The future didn't exist. Only the here and now. The last few hours of hair-raising and extremely taxing sailing were beginning to take on a tinge of unreality, as if the experience hadn't been so bad after all.

There are few recollections that have remained so clear and intense in my mind as those I have from being at sea and in port after a long and demanding voyage. And of them all, the memory of our arrival in Fraserburgh in *Rustica* is the clearest and sharpest.

'*Sometimes*,' Harry Martinson says very simply in *Cape Farewell*, '*the sea seemed to me a dream, so close to reality did I live.*'

On vagrancy

In a special issue of *Svensk Juristtidning* (Swedish Law Journal) in 1937, a *festschrift* for Ernst Trygger, the attentive reader will find an article by K. Schluyter with the somewhat ambiguous title 'The competent authority in vagrancy cases'. The author discusses the proposals that had been put forward at the time for a revision – long-awaited, one assumes – of the vagrancy law of 1885.

Schluyter introduces his argument with an account of the new draft law, 'according to which some recidivist criminals (as well as some first offenders) could be sentenced to detention in a workhouse when there was a presumption that their criminality was principally a manifestation of or adjunct to *their inclination to an indolent or unsettled lifestyle*' (author's italics). He continues: 'The detainee could be held in the institution for a relatively indeterminate length of time, although a minimum period of one or two years and a maximum of two or four years should be set, according to the nature of the individual case, with the option in both instances of extension by one year, dependent on the result of release on parole'. Later in the same article Schluyter cites Thyrén (only identified by surname) as the expert having coined the immediately intelligible concept of 'criminality by reason of indolence'. It should be noted that the new law was intended to form part of the penal code.

Nowadays we can perhaps smile at this. But more particularly we can note the inherent contradiction in sentencing the homeless to custody in an institution, in other words to a roof over their heads, and then to release them on parole, presumably to homelessness.

What is clear, however, is that a considerable number of long-distance sailors and other dreamers would have fallen foul of this law if it had been in force today. For what sailor would not want to live an 'indolent life' in the warmth, cooled only by the shade of palm trees, the trade-wind and the crystal-clear turquoise waters of the oceans?

Nevertheless we can observe, and rejoice in, the fact that things are somewhat improved in a few respects in this world of ours. It is frequently asserted that mankind is incorrigible, fundamentally evil and profoundly selfish. Seen in this light, common humanity would be a luxury, something we could employ or discard as the fancy took us. George Orwell's response to this view was that we had at least abolished cannibalism. We can now add to this, that an indolent life is no longer a criminal offence.

Yet society still shows no great comprehension of those who evince little enthusiasm for permanent employment and a settled life on land. Nor is it particularly sympathetic towards anyone who is lunatic enough to want to live on a boat. There are countless stories of long-distance sailors having problems with officialdom and other petty despots when they have openly and honestly admitted their intentions of foregoing their rightful share of the fruits of civilisation for a year or two.

I personally never cease to be surprised at the widespread inability to concede that there can be *exceptions to the rule*, for instance to the cherished assumption that everyone is best off living in a house that conforms to all the building regulations and standards of health and occupancy.

Sweden is (in)famous for its bureaucracy, but as far as our residence on a boat was concerned, I have to say that we had many more problems in Denmark. All I had to do in Sweden was to register myself by putting a cross on a pre-printed form and choosing a postbox address at any post office, and I would be enrolled for tax purposes in the same district. As far as I understand, there is no law in Sweden compelling us to have a fixed abode or firm ground beneath our feet.

It is completely different in Denmark. Helle began by ringing the local council to ask what she should do about living on a boat. On the first occasion she was told to phone back. When she did so, she could not get any answer to her question, but was simply referred from one person to another. When she said the boat was Swedish-ensigned and that it had no fixed home port, there was complete silence at the other end. Some office pen-pusher started talking about a seaman's book, which might indeed have been advantageous from the taxation aspect, but was completely impossible in view of the fact that Helle had her own company and worked and received a salary in Copenhagen.

In the end it became rather Kafkaesque – she spoke to yet another pen-pusher who tried to advise her against living on a boat, particularly a boat without a permanent home port and peripatetic between various harbours in the Öresund and on Sjælland: 'Living on a boat like that can be dangerous!'

'Dangerous?' repeated Helle, taken aback.

'Yes, what if the boat were outside your council area and you fell ill? It would be a long way to hospital.'

'Well, in that case it would be just as dangerous to visit my aunt in Fredriksborg, wouldn't it?' Helle asked.

Which brought the immediate sententious response, 'You probably don't do that very often.' But in fact, Helle both had an aunt in Fredriksborg and had worked in Hilleröd, not far from there. She had travelled back and forth between her job in Hilleröd and Copenhagen without any official finding cause to tell her how 'dangerous' it might be. And think of all the people who commute daily between Helsingør and Copenhagen. Or even worse, between Helsingør and Helsingborg, in Sweden, between home and abroad. Commuters such as these took their lives in their hands every single day!

After many attempts and even more referrals to other numbers Helle finally got hold of a senior member of staff, actually the director of the council tax department.

'Why not just get a pro-forma address ashore?' he suggested. 'Then there won't be a problem.'

'In that case, can I choose the cheapest council area?' Helle asked.

'Why not? That's what I would do.'

~

So we solved the problem of being vagabonds and seafarers in enlightened Scandinavia. I lived in a postbox for a number of years and Helle lived pro-forma. Not that we minded. On the contrary. Not everyone is privileged to live in a postbox, after all. The postmistress even shed an emotional tear when I told her I was moving; I was the post office's only tenant. But the sad thing is that officialdom, like an autopilot, doesn't know what to do with exceptions to the rule.

Although fundamentally it was about something quite different, of course: the settled person's fear of the traveller, or as Harry Martinson put it:

> Everything that is redolent of the nomad is anathema to the truly repressed, who view it as indecent and anti-social. I, believing in the opposing religion of the itinerant, am convinced of the universal social obligation of being footloose, especially where the well-being of the soul is at stake.
>
> (*Aimless Travels*)

For that very reason it should be accepted as selfevident, just as it was for Martinson, that

travelling is a basic human right.

On living aboard a small boat, especially in winter

It must have been one January that Helle and I invited her mother, her sisters and their husbands to dinner on board. When they came at about six it was dark. We were berthed as usual behind the northern stone wall of the old harbour of Dragør, the little fishing and ferry port immediately south of Copenhagen and Kastrup airport, more or less the only boat there. The temperature outside was minus five Celsius. Inside it was between ten and thirty degrees, depending on whether you were near the floor or up at ceiling level. Our oil stove gave out a generous heat, but unevenly distributed.

We spent the whole evening in the cheerful atmosphere of the saloon, talking, drinking wine and eating as well as at any time on land. The wind was a light westerly, so all that could be heard was a faint lapping against *Rustica*'s hull. It was only when there was a strong east or south-east wind that we ever rolled. The evening passed, it was soon midnight and time for them to go home. When we came up on deck we found a four-inch layer of snow on the deck and the jetties. Everything was still. The wind had dropped completely. We stood gazing raptly out over the Öresund with its lighthouses winking in the darkness. A magical scene.

~

Once I actually saw the ice forming. I was in the cabin looking out of the porthole. That night there was a light clear northerly breeze blowing from the Arctic. I watched some gulls perched on the mooring piles with their heads turned as always into the wind. As I stood there the little wind-ripples started to disappear and the water soon looked as if it were covered with oil. Only then did it strike me that what I was witnessing was the first ice forming a thin membrane on the dark surface and it was this membrane that was making the ripples subside. When we woke the next morning the ice had thickened enough to bear the weight of a tern standing shivering beside the boat.

The ice came late that winter and seemed to surprise many of the seabirds that were already finding it difficult to feed themselves in the cold; the terns seemed particularly affected. One clear sunny morning we saw a tern freeze to death on the ice by the boat. It stood there motionless all morning staring in the same direction, oblivious to the wind blowing its feathers open and letting in even more cold. By midday it couldn't take any more and keeled over.

It was a heart-rending sight, but who were we to interfere with nature?

～

It must have been the beginning of March when we suffered one of the worst storms for a century. I was working at the time in Eslöv across the water in Sweden and from my window there I could see the trees bending in the gale. The news reported chaos on the roads and winds of up to seventy-five miles an hour, virtually hurricane-force, at Kastrup airport in Copenhagen. All flights had been cancelled. The ferries were confined to port and those that hadn't been able to make it into harbour had hove to. I had trouble concentrating on my work, worrying about *Rustica*. But at least I knew that Helle had left the boat and gone to work before the worst of the gale.

I went home earlier than usual that day. I took the first ferry out of Limhamn after the morning's disruption of service. It was still blowing so hard that the captain had to use the anchor to manoeuvre in harbour.

In Dragør everything was normal. Apart from the seaweed on the jetty there was nothing to indicate that there had been an almighty storm only a few hours before. Even the stove was burning exactly as usual and *Rustica*'s cabin was warm and inviting.

When Helle came home at six the wind had died down to a stiff breeze. The sky was cloudless and spangled with stars. It was chilly, but there was every indication that we would be able to sleep in peace and quiet instead of having to sit up on watch as we had feared.

After dinner I went up on deck for a while to look out over the Öresund, where the winking light- houses were clearly visible against the now almost perfectly calm water. The wind had practically died away. What a change of scene! I noticed the water had risen about six inches, which was not that uncommon. Despite the lack of tides, the water always rose in Dragør in strong northerly winds.

Two hours later, half an hour before midnight, I looked out again. The water had risen even more, a disturbing amount. The mooring ropes were pointing downwards. Only three or four inches of the piles astern showed above the surface, as against the normal couple of feet. At the bows the water was lapping over the jetty. I went out and slackened off the ropes.

Helle retired to bed, but I was too concerned to sleep. Just as well. The sea carried on rising. By one o'clock the jetties were totally submerged. The ropes on neighbouring boats were as taut as violin strings. Since buoyancy is greatest at the stern and least at the bows, they were all pointing downwards. Palle, a friend who had his boat overwintering in the harbour, turned up at half past one in waders and struggled out into the water and up on to his boat to loosen off the mooring ropes. The pilot boat opposite looked as if it was moored in the middle of the sea, with its mooring ropes at an angle of forty-five degrees. The pilot had to be rowed to it so that he could get out to a vessel which needed piloting through the Sound.

The water finally turned at half past two in the morning. By then it was not only the jetties that had disappeared, but even the stone wall that was meant to protect us from wind and storm. When I looked out I could see the whole of the Öresund before me, a weird sensation, as if we too were moored out at sea. It certainly was the greatest good fortune there was not a breath of wind by then. I hardly dared think what would have happened if the gale had continued.

We heard next morning that large parts of Dragør had been flooded and that the water had risen more than 1.3 metres in six hours. The port electricity supply had been flooded and cut. We had to live without mains electricity for a month. Not that it bothered us. We had decided from the beginning that we ought to be able to manage without electricity.

~

We spent five winters on *Rustica*, four of them in Dragør and one in Kinsale. We would not have missed the experience for anything. We still talk about winter days when the north wind from the Arctic swept in and gave infinite visibility, when the low winter sun sparkled on the snow on the jetty, or, somewhat less amusing, when I fell in the water as I took rubbish ashore one January morning or the occasion Helle caught her rucksack in the forestay and was suspended with one leg on *Rustica* and the other on land.

So there was beauty, drama and comedy to life on board. But above all there was a peacefulness and a concentration on certain basic values that it is not easy to attain ashore. It was a healthy contrast to work on land. Nowhere else can I relax the way I can on the boat and forget about all the things that have to be done, all the meetings to be attended, all the papers to be read and written, all the clocks that divide up our time to no purpose, all the men in suits going around looking important, all the conflicts and petty intrigues.

Just being without television, telephone, daily newspaper and daily post with all its obligations leaves you free for other more life-enhancing activities.

I like books and own a great many. One of the supreme advantages of life ashore is that you can cover the bare walls of your house with books. You can't, of course, in a boat. For one thing you don't want to conceal richly-varnished wood with book spines, and secondly there isn't the space. We had room for five feet of personal books each and another six feet for books on yachts and navigation. We missed being able to scan our shelves hunting out something to read on a dull rainy Sunday in November. But we learnt to value what we had, carefully selected works that stood up to re-reading. One tip for those who live on board ship or make long voyages: start learning a foreign language. A grammar, a decent dictionary, a few thick novels and a couple of other texts will last for ever. In Swedish I would have read *A Hundred Years of Solitude* and *Don Quixote* in a few days. In Spanish, which I had been teaching myself for ten years, it took several months. And what reading experiences! I have seldom read a text so closely.

But lovers of order, whether sailors or not, are probably interested primarily in how it can be possible to live year-round on a boat at all, rain or shine, hot or cold, in calm or storm. Because apart from sceptical smiles and shakes of the head, it is principally questions of a practical nature that we get asked when we say we used to live on a boat, without an apartment or a house ashore as a back-up.

'Isn't it cold?'

'What do you do about a shower?'

'Can you have a telephone on board?'

'Or TV?' 'How do you do the washing?'

'What happens when it's icy?'

'Isn't it damp?'

These are some of the more prosaic questions we have had about life on board. Very few people, remarkably few, have asked about the poetry of living on a boat.

It would not be difficult to write an entire volume about what is needed to live on a boat all year round at our latitudes. I don't intend to do it. But since this book is meant to be partially a source of inspiration for realistic dreams, a few important pieces of practical advice may not go amiss.

So, cold and damp.

Before we moved on board permanently we took a number of steps which together turned out to function better than we could ever have hoped, with some minor exceptions.

Heating first. We decided at an early stage to manage entirely without alternating current from land, and even without direct current batteries. So we bought a Reflex diesel-burning stove and installed three good-sized paraffin lamps, of which one, a stainless-steel Stelton lamp, emits as much light as a 40-watt bulb plus 700 watts of heat. In the installation instructions for the Reflex they recommended that the air intake should be connected by a pipe to a deck vent to avoid the risk of lack of oxygen inside the boat. We chose to ignore the advice, since we had installed no fewer than six vents in the deck and another four air intakes in the cubby-hole in the cockpit. Our rejection of the instructions turned out to be a triumph. What happened was that the stove greedily sucked in all the cold damp air at floor level and sent it out up the chimney. And it speeded up the air circulation so that we got a faint draught all the time from stem to stern. This single – and elementary – measure did more than anything else to keep the boat warm and dry.

There were really only two disadvantages: candles flickered and dripped, and there was a smell of food in the forepeak, our bedroom, for several hours after dinner. It was a small price to pay for keeping warm and dry. Our second step was to line the boat with insulation, not the usual three to five millimetres, but a centimetre-thick foam sheet with a high thermal coefficient, like the sort used as a bed-roll for hiking or in tents. Our initial idea was to stick it on with adhesive, and we did this for the ceiling, but then we realised that in stowage spaces and cupboards we could just cut it slightly oversized and push it into place. That too was a success, because the inevitable condensation which formed on the inside of the hull just ran down into the bilges behind the insulation.

Finally, we painted the insulation on the outside with moisture-absorbing paint. If the paint was effective on submarines and icebreakers, which it evidently was, it ought to work in an over-wintering fibreglass yacht.

It did, beyond all expectations, although its surface was not particularly beautiful and it was troublesome to keep neat and clean. But the main thing was that our clothes could be kept in the wardrobe for weeks without going mouldy or starting to smell (not too much, anyway).

So we coped with damp and cold, down to minus ten or even lower if there was no north wind.

All the other things you need for living on a boat during the winter are really minor details.We used a launderette to wash our clothes and bedding once a fortnight. Our mail came to a postbox number, to Helle's pro-forma address or to work. There were telephone kiosks if we needed faster communication. Nowadays, with mobile phones, the 'problem' of wireless communication in both directions is – unfortunately – just a memory. It is worth mentioning, however, that I scarcely ever had complaints from friends and acquaintances about our 'inaccessibility' despite the fact that they couldn't simply lift the receiver to get hold of us (perhaps it should be emphasised that there is still no law against not having a telephone; I lived for ten years myself, even on land, without a phone – and it was superb).

Ice can be a concern, especially in the thaw and particularly if you choose to live in a caulked wooden boat. The damp in the cotton which is driven in between the boards freezes and is liable to seep out when the ice starts to melt in spring. A square-hulled fibreglass motorboat would also have problems because its straight sides might be crushed by the ice. But for a deep rounded boat with a keel the water is several degrees warmer below the keel and that warmth is drawn up through the hull, and the rounded shape means that the hull cannot stick fast in the ice. If the boat is also heated to twenty degrees there is no risk whatsoever. We heard of a sailor who lived on an Allegro during one of the worst winters of the 1980s. The ice was three feet thick in harbour, but the boat froze fast only on a couple of nights. And the hull was normally surrounded by a strip of slush.

The sole drawback for a heated yacht is that the boat is usually heated in the stem, but not in the stern under the cockpit. This means that the ice melts at the bows, which makes the boat slowly and inexorably ease forward. You have to go out from time to time and saw out a hole astern and move the boat back so that you don't snap your moorings. That's all, and the problem doesn't arise of course if you have a heated aft cabin.

No, the greatest hurdles to overcome for all-year-round life afloat are not on the technical or practical side. They relate to the people who live in the vessel. But there is no shame in not wishing to live in a fibreglass box through the winter, ready to sail anywhere at a moment's notice. It must be a very small minority who want to have the perpetual possibility of getting away from everything.

That's the way it is with wanderlust. Most people have it, but secreted in a dark recess which is only revealed when it is too late.

We express our deepest wanderlust with our feet and legs. The itchy feet of restlessness call, 'sell all you own and come follow me'. And so we may begin our travels to and fro across a floor of a hundred square feet, four steps to and fro in a prison cell, or a globetrotter trip across the Sahara.

(*Aimless Travels*)

But for most people it is probably the four steps that are important, even if preferably in a terraced house or a package-holiday hotel rather than a prison cell.

Which is fortunate, because overcrowded winter harbours would lose their charm. At least for me.

On sailing by tide or on dry land
or not at all

The first time we sailed without water was in Brittany, on the way into Paimpol. Everything was green on our Admiralty chart, a sure sign of land. We took yet another look at our calculations and at the clock. Had we calculated correctly? All the times in the tide tables were given in GMT for English harbours. For the French harbours they gave GMT+1, French winter time. But now it was summer, which ought to be GMT+2, surely?

It was three nautical miles to the security and relief of the lock in Paimpol, about half an hour's sailing. What depth was there? Would the tide be high enough to get us to the lock? Around Paimpol the difference between high and low tide could be as much as ten metres.

That first attempt of ours to sail without water turned out well. We arrived at the lock at high tide and were admitted after only a short wait. Two hours later the port of Paimpol was completely cut off from the sea. Where we had sailed there were several miles of muddy ground. The red and green buoys lying here and there marked a non-existent channel that had been reduced to a dry ditch, a dredged furrow without which Paimpol would not have been accessible by sea at all.

For people like us, Swedes and Danes, it is a very strange experience to discover that the water incessantly rises and falls. It is particularly extreme in northern Brittany. Around St-Malo the difference between high and low tide can be up to twelve metres, as much as a four-storey building.

People drown every year from venturing out to the exposed areas without local knowledge and finding their retreat suddenly cut off. The strong currents swirling in the deeper parts are often impossible to swim against.

It goes without saying that sailing in waters such as these is an unusual experience for us, compared with waters back home in Scandinavia. Anchoring, for instance. To be safe the general rule is to lay out cable to a length corresponding to five times your depth. But what do you do when there is a difference of ten metres between high and low tide and you 'only' have a sixty metre cable? Well, you realise straight away that you can never anchor in water deeper than two metres at low tide – if you want to keep within safety margins. The problem of course is finding a protected anchorage with a depth of two metres. So you have to have a chain, or chain and rope, of more than sixty metres (we ourselves have eighty metres).

The next difficulty is that the tide only runs in the same direction for six hours, after which it turns and runs the opposite way. That means that after a few hours the boat will swing round with the tidal current, irrespective of the wind direction. In English it's called being 'tide-ridden' instead of 'wind-ridden', which latter is the norm in non-tidal waters. If the boat has a short keel, if the current is weak and the wind strong, you can probably get by, but otherwise the boat inevitably swings through 180 degrees on every change of tide. If you have a long keel like *Rustica* and the current is running at more than two knots, the wind speed is irrelevant. The result is that most anchors break loose before they – with luck – find a new hold. So a sensible skipper ought to wake up every six hours ('wake' because the tide turns in the middle of the night as well, of course), go up on deck and check that the anchor really is biting after the tide has turned. But checking your bearings in pitch darkness can be tricky, often with no lights ashore. After all, you would very often have chosen an anchorage at a decent distance from the marvels of civilisation, including street lamps. Another factor in northern Brittany is that most anchorages are in rivers where the tidal current is extra strong.

But it is not just lying at anchor that is difficult. Sailing can be just as fraught. At least when you have a yacht capable of no more than six knots under favourable conditions.

In many places the current runs at four or five knots for several hours. It can even reach nine knots, for example in the Alderney Races between Alderney and Cap de la Hague in Normandy, in Le Raz de Sein between the west coast of Brittany and the Ile de Sein, in the Chenal du Four between the Ile d'Ouessant and the mainland, and round the Ile de Bréhat in northern Brittany. There is no question of sailing into the wind and into the current, not at least if your intention is to make any headway.

But nor is it certain that sailing against the current even *with* the wind is possible. The current can be faster than the speed the wind can give the boat, however much following wind you have. It is called wind over tide.

And if there is one thing a sailor should avoid like the plague, it is wind over tide. So there remains only one alternative: with the wind and with the current. How often do they coincide? Not as often as we would like, anyway. When it does occasionally happen, then you really get up speed, at least for the six hours you have before the tide turns again. Even we, with our average best of no more than five knots, have sometimes managed to make ten knots and sixty nautical miles in six hours.

～

I have twice sailed through Le Raz de Blanchard, or the Alderney Races as it's called in English, the sound between Alderney and the French mainland. On a spring tide, those days every month when the difference between high and low water is greatest, the current here can get up to an unbelievable ten knots for several hours. And it runs through fairly shallow seas over an uneven floor, which means that bodies of water are not just moving horizontally but also vertically. This can give rise to races and overfalls, areas where short, steep waves break with or without wind.

There were warnings about the Alderney Races in all our navigation books. First and foremost you had to have the tide with you even to contemplate a passage. Secondly the headwind shouldn't be more than twenty miles an hour if you didn't want to risk your life. Preferably, of course, you should have both tide and wind with you. And finally you should avoid sailing on a spring tide, when the tidal current is at its strongest.

We chose a day without any wind at all, even if we couldn't avoid a spring tide. Five boats sailed out of Cherbourg at the same time as us, bound for the Alderney Races. They must all have been in their respective cabins calculating and come up with the same result. You had to be at a certain point a certain number of hours after high tide at Cherbourg if you wanted to be sure of taking advantage of a favourable current right through the Races. There was no alternative. If you were halfway through when the tide turned you would inevitably be flushed out into the English Channel again.

What our pilot books had omitted to mention was that there were races and overfalls on the way to the given starting position, probably because relatively speaking they were not dangerous. So, exactly like the other yachts, we were caught napping when the calm seas suddenly began to seethe without the slightest warning. *Moana* leapt and bounced so that the outboard motor raced every time the propeller came out of the water. A young helmsman on a nearby boat was panic-stricken and instinctively tried to escape by turning through 180 degrees, the result of which was a near-collision with us.

But the current quickly carried us over the turbulent patch, and at two o'clock we were exactly where we should have been. We switched off the motor and hoisted the sail to test it. It filled well so we let ourselves be drawn into the straits in silence.

But after a while we began to wonder if everything was all right. Janne took a bearing from the lighthouse on shore and couldn't get it to agree with our reckoning. I repeated the experiment without success. A feeling of uncertainty established itself on board until after much discussion we concluded that the boat had turned round and we were being pushed backwards at ten knots. And there wasn't any wind. The sails were simply being filled by our own motion as the current swept *Moana* with it through the still air. We started the motor in order at least to have our bows pointing in the right direction.

We soon sailed into mist that reduced visibility to a couple of nautical miles. We never even caught a glimpse of Jersey, only five nautical miles to port. We kept track of where we were with the radio direction finder and my plotting of tide vectors.

We managed to pass Jersey before it was time for the tide to change. After that all danger of being sucked back was over. South of Jersey the current runs in an east-west direction at about two knots, which suited us fine because it got us away from Les Minquiers, a perilous area with rocks just beneath the surface. (If you want some idea of what it is like, I advise you to read Hammond Innes' book *The Wreck of the Mary Deare*.)

The return was not so successful. We had to get up at five in the morning to fit in with the tide. We were in Guernsey, closer to the Alderney Races from that direction than Cherbourg was from the other. We passed through the lock at six a.m. with a dozen yachts heading the same way. There were a couple of friendly Frenchmen standing on the quay wishing us *bon voyage*. We had the impression they were slightly worried about us with our small boat and relative youth. They themselves were from Normandy and had sailed these waters all their lives, and if there was anything they had respect for it was the Alderney Races. Their rule was quite simply never to sail through in a headwind.

Once out of the lock we hoisted sail and motored for a while, as did the others, though they drew ahead with their bigger engines. Exactly as before we sailed without warning into an area of overfalls that made us ship water into the cockpit. *Moana* reared up like an unruly horse. Immediately after that the wind increased somewhat and since we were fed up with the outboard motor racing as soon as we were in choppy seas, we switched it off and continued under sail alone. We fell further and further behind the rest of the pack, who kept going at full speed under power. That was our mistake. When the tide turned six hours later we were not yet on the safe side of it, even though we had got past the place where the tidal stream ran at its wildest. The result was that we sailed for another six hours at five knots under both sail and power, but without making an inch of headway; if anything, we went backwards.

It was a hair-raising experience. Who could tell whether we could hold our own and at least maintain our position? Great was our relief when the current at first imperceptibly then ever more noticeably loosened its grip and let us sail on to Cherbourg.

Brittany is full of such dangerous and highly unpredictable straits. The entire west coast is bristling with rocks, swirling currents and various kinds of races, the currents that are produced when tidal streams meet uneven seabed. The worst two places are round the windswept islands of Ouessant and Sein. There is an old sailors' rhyme about them, spoken, not sung:

Qui voit Ouessant, voit son sang.
Qui voit Ile de Sein, voit sa fin.
(If you see Ouessant, you see your blood.
If you see the Ile de Sein, you see your end.)

Bretons themselves who have sailed round the world say that if you can sail in Brittany you can sail anywhere. There is something in that. When Peter Blake and his crew beat the world record for a non-stop circumnavigation of the globe, they ran into a storm verging on a hurricane just as they sailed in over the continental shelf on the approach to Ouessant. Once in harbour they were unanimous that it was the only time on the whole voyage that they had feared for life and limb. They had never seen such seas as there.

So it is hardly surprising that the majority of France's famous yachtsmen and seamen come from Brittany. From one point of view. Though we may wonder why Bretons have chosen to seek a living on such treacherous and dangerous seas at all. One explanation is that they never had much choice. Not that the land was barren or stony. Brittany is an important agricultural region nowadays, even if not for grain. No, the reason is rather that the Bretons were poor and exploited by rich and predominantly French landowners. Land has always cost money. The sea costs nothing.

In St-Malo it was even forbidden for people living within the walls to own land outside. So the Malouins were forced out into freedom and took the whole world as their workplace. For the boys and young men of St-Malo running along the quayside when the fishing fleet, corsairs and West Indiamen were preparing for sea, one of life's fundamental problems was solved: how to fulfil their dreams. It was different for girls. The most they could dream of was to marry a man who would survive the sea. For what was the stake freedom demanded, if not life?

But are such sentiments anything but romantic drivel? What freedom did the fishermen and seamen really have? Their lives were gruelling. It was a constant battle to put food on the table, and usually not much more than that. The so-called ordinary seamen who sailed with the great explorers and adventurers did not have a lot to hope for, whether on this side of the grave or beyond. Their only freedom was that of the dreamer.

I had gone to sea infatuated with adolescent romantic dreams of pirates and Red Indians. And the sea roared, romantically, sexlessly, 'Adventure! Adventure! Out and plunder!'

But new sights, new ideas, new dreams. Events changed me, and not I them as in a fairy tale. I had at first to minister to the caprices of a little steam boiler, bracing my muscles in my carefully orchestrated work, and vomit into the coal, feeling ill and anxious, on a little bouncing three-hundred-tonner in the North Atlantic.

(*Aimless Travels*)

On the art of compromise and the middle way

All books about long-distance sailing, indeed about sailing of any kind, discuss boats. What boat shall I choose if I want to sail long distance? Should it have a long keel or short keel? Should it be single- or multi-hulled? Is it better to have a light boat that will veer away from waves or a heavy one that can take a pounding? Should it have a masthead rig or 7/8 rig? What sort of stern should it have, vertical transom, canoe stern, scoop transom or counter stern? Should it be fast so that you have time to seek shelter before an approaching storm? Or slow so that you're not racing the waves? And the hull material? Fibreglass, steel, aluminium, ferro-cement or wood? This is the stuff of quayside conversation.

What is remarkable is that questions such as these have not found conclusive answers. Nor are they ever likely to.

Nearly all vessels are built for the waters they are to sail in and for the loads they will carry. For a long time British-built yachts were under-rigged in comparison with their Swedish counterparts. This is because Britain is surrounded by merciless seas, whereas Swedes mostly sail in the lee of skerries where they need high-masted sails to catch whatever breeze there is.

Both in Kinsale, on the south coast of Ireland, and in Galway, on the west coast, people used to build a type of boat called a hooker. But the Kinsale hooker fished in open and unprotected seas, when it wasn't making smuggling trips to Brittany, whereas the Galway hooker had to plough its way through the choppy seas behind the Aran Islands outside

Galway Bay that break up the eternally booming swell of the Atlantic. So one hooker was broad and stable, a toad like the Colin Archer, whereas the other was deep, narrow and sleek.

I met an acquaintance one day in St-Malo: Christian, a captain for Brittany Ferries, the company operating between St-Malo and Portsmouth, who had just returned from Trelleborg in Sweden, where he had spent a week inspecting and test-sailing the Baltic ferry *Nils Holgersson*, which Brittany Ferries had purchased. He told me the ship would have to be rebuilt at a cost of several hundred thousand pounds before it could venture out into the English Channel. Stability had to be improved, the bows sharpened and much else. As she stood, she was simply not sufficiently seaworthy to take out on a real sea. So indeed it is: the ferries that sail out of the Swedish Baltic ports as floating hotels, pleasure palaces and shopping malls are only built for the Baltic. And tragically enough, not even always that.

Take the *Queen of Scandinavia*, a deformed box, acquired by a Danish ferry line from the Sweden–Finland route, whose snout of a prow seems only to be there for show, whose height above the waterline makes her look as if she would tip over if you so much as gave her a poke. Compare that misshapen hull with the regal old *King of Scandinavia*, a long, slender and gorgeous vessel by any standards, a real passenger liner, well-proportioned, elegant and fit for its purpose.

It used to be said that boats should be beautiful in order to sail well, meaning that aesthetics and functionality were two sides of the same coin. That, of course, like so much else, is a truth in need of qualification. Which is the chicken and which the egg? It is possible that sailors want to believe a boat that sails like a dream matches up to that dream in its looks. Or vice versa. Few yachts are prettier than a *knarr* or a Folkboat, but without self-draining cockpits they have no place on the open sea. Yet they sail well and are a pleasure to watch. And it's true to say that a vessel built for all waters, or for no particular waters at all, is at best a serviceable compromise, at worst an ugly and useless monstrosity.

It has often been asserted, to the point of becoming a well-worn cliché, that a sailing yacht is always a compromise. There is more truth to the statement than may at first appear. Because the fact is that there is no ideal compromise, one that would offer a synthesis of the best qualities of all types of yacht. Boatbuilders seem to be in agreement on one thing: that a craft cannot be designed for both racing and cruising, for windward and downwind, for canals and oceans, for space and beauty, at least not if it is to be the optimum for each and every purpose. We could say there is no such thing as an optimal boat.

Let us look at some examples. *Rustica* is a longkeeled yacht, but the keel is actually rather short, which is to say that it starts quite a way astern. This means she beats to windward well and tacks easily. Vessels from earlier days, for instance the famous Bristol cutter, had keels that started right up at the bows and continued back the whole length of the boat. They beat to windward nowhere near as effectively as modern long-keeled yachts, and their manoeuvrability was not very impressive. Though they lay at anchor well, without blowing from one side to the other in gusts. And they rode the waves well when they were hove to. Nor did they run the risk of falling over when you let them stand out of water to scrape their hulls. But like all long-keeled yachts, including *Rustica*, they are hopeless when reversing under power.

In other words, designing a boat with optimum performance both at anchor and under sail is an impossibility. That doesn't mean there are not boats that are better or worse than others. There are some compromises that function more successfully than others.

In many languages the word compromise has developed negative connotations, meaning something that could have been better. In politics, in art, in human relationships, a compromise is seen as a halfbaked, makeshift solution, something we have to live with for lack of anything more satisfactory. Democracy, for instance, is said to be a compromise, the least bad system of government.

That view, I venture to suggest, is not merely wrongheaded, it is dangerous. Mankind and interpersonal relationships are infinitely complex, much more so than a boat's relationship to wind and waves. The belief that there is one simple and uniform solution to mankind's problems can only be wishful thinking or blindness.

'*Never a middle way*,' says Harry Martinson in *Cape Farewell*, and continues:

> Warmongers and Stock Exchange barons know no middle way. The middle way is the way of reason, and also of the truest ecstasy and emotion. Ecstasy should belong to us, not to machines. To hell with the rapture of the threshing-mill. We do not feel it in our veins and in our souls: all it does is torture and destroy us with its lifeless, empty din.

'*Civilisation*,' he also writes, '*is the cultivation of the essential middle ways, which can form a basis for ecstasy and happiness.*'

It wouldn't surprise me a jot if one of the primary reasons why Martinson has been regarded by lesser writers and lesser people as a spineless reactionary and technophobic softie was because he always sang the praises of the middle way. Middle ways and compromises! How grey and boring! No, we like strong opinions!

But these critics of Harry Martinson have not understood anything. They have not grasped the power and beauty inherent in his middle way. Yet he has explained himself with as much clarity as anyone could wish:

> Our ideal should be not the calm, which can turn the very ocean to a stagnant pool, nor the hurricane, but the mighty trade-wind, fresh, life-giving and unfailing.

Most ideologies are at the extremes of either gale-force or total calm, presumably to attract attention. What political party or programme can be compared to the moderation and stability of the trade-winds? None as far as I am aware. Who would vote for the 'Compromise Party'? Nobody I know.

There is much work to do for the enterprising and energetic as far as middle way trade-winds are concerned.

On Celts and rings on the water

The Ile de Groix is off the south coast of Brittany. It has remained somewhat in the shadow of its idyllic neighbour, which presumes to call itself Belle Ile, Beautiful Island. The Ile de Groix is perhaps best known as a paradise for stone enthusiasts such as myself. Nowhere else in France have so many different minerals been found in so small an area. The island is geologically so unique that removing stones is totally prohibited.

But even if you are not a stone collector the Ile de Groix has much to offer, except in the French holiday month of August. There is a good protected harbour on the north side, behind a lock. The little town is delightful, even if wanting in basic facilities for sailors, particularly a grocer's shop and ship chandler's. But you can buy fresh bread in one of the cafés, of which there are plenty, as there are of bars.

We made our choice, a cross between fishermen's pub and hippie café. The bar was run by a former Breton fisherman, aged about forty, who had changed horses. As I drank my beer I noticed there were postcards of Scotland on the walls and Irish music playing. I said I had sailed in both Scotland and Ireland and that from Brittany I was en route to Galicia. He said he had fished a lot round Scotland and Ireland and that the Bretons had always got on well with them up there. Quite different from the English, he added, unsolicited. I asked him whether he thought Brittany had something special in common with Scotland and Ireland. His answer was that they were 'all Celtic countries' and that they had always belonged together across the sea. But he didn't feel the same affinity with the Galicians. They were Spaniards, he said, not Celts.

∼

I was berthed in Howth, part of Dublin, gathering my strength for my imminent solo passage. I can't say I liked it there. Howth is a fashionable suburb, perhaps one of the few really fashionable suburbs in the whole of Ireland, and the yacht club is a *yacht* club, not just a sailing club. Howth was actually the only place in Ireland where I didn't manage to get to know the locals, if there were such a category in Howth. The problem with these haunts for the rich is that no one comes there for any reason except the proximity of other wealthy people. It is not particularly conducive to communal activities.

Typically enough, the only individuals I came in contact with were visiting yachtsmen like myself. I moored alongside a yellow Sparksman & Stephens named *Rebel*. Unfortunately it had a large Confederate flag painted on the stern, which made me doubtful about the potential company. But I was not too prejudiced to respond to a greeting, and from the first conversation learnt that John and Susan had only recently bought their boat and had not painted the flag themselves; in fact they more or less apologised for sailing around with it still on. I was invited aboard for a drink that same evening. They were from England, but kept their boat in Holyhead, the big ferry port on Anglesey, for the simple reason that they liked sailing to Ireland as often as they could. They shared with all the other non-Irish I met a love of Ireland and the Irish. They thought there was no more hospitable country. But, explained John, keeping the boat in Wales was a high price to pay. He recounted the difficulties and minor hassles they had experienced. Then he said forcibly, 'I don't like that race!'

So the Welsh are a race?

∼

I have already written about Canna, an idyllic island anchorage, at least in good weather, between the Inner and Outer Hebrides. It was on Canna that we met Gordon and discovered Runrig, Runrig first and Gordon second.

Runrig is a Scottish rock group who sing and write music in English and Gaelic. Their music is magnificent, light and airy, rhythmic and political. Their music proves that Scotland has a right to its name and its own life. It is also a homage to a majestic landscape. When Runrig music wafted out of Gordon's cabin across the calm waters of Canna, it seemed to belong there.

It was through Runrig that we got to know him; he was the man who subscribed ten pounds a month to the National Trust to preserve Scotland's heritage, despite himself having trouble making ends meet.

The day we met him he had been ashore to visit the island's ruined church. What struck me was his wholehearted commitment to his own roots and Scotland's history. He had a profound sense of where he belonged.

~

In *The Celtic Ring* I told the story of our meeting with a young Scot whose name I didn't remember. He borrowed some lures from us to fish (illegally), and we then invited him on board *Rustica* for a whisky in the cabin. We talked about national character, though our young guest didn't use that term. He expressed his loathing, albeit with a paradoxically warm humour, for most of the foreigners who came to Scotland: the Americans, the English (above all), and southerners in general. And he had a real grudge against the Lowlanders, who had sold Scotland to the English. When we asked him if there were any people he could tolerate, he replied immediately, 'The Irish!'

'Why?' we asked.

'They're genuine.'

The discussion turned to the mysterious ruin, Invergarry Castle, in the shadow of which we were moored. We expressed our sorrow that it had burnt down in a clan war three hundred years ago. Our guest was indignant and said it should have been razed to the ground. It had been built by a clan that had sided with the English and had no right to be there.

We were left in no doubt that his anger was deep-felt. For him three hundred years was no time at all. If he had been able to write French he would have described his history in the *passé composé* and not the *passé simple*. The former treats history as still living in the present, the latter severs all connection with what has gone before.

~

We were in Lochboisdale on South Uist in the Outer Hebrides. It was very blustery, a stiff breeze from the south-east. We were safely moored to one of the buoys provided here and there by the Scottish Highlands Board for visiting yachts. They are free and guaranteed to hold fifteen tons. After a week at anchor it is so good to tie up to a buoy and not have to be continually taking bearings to check that you're still in the same place. Our only misfortune was that Lochboisdale is partly open to the south-east, so the sea was rolling in and keeping us on board for fear that the dinghy would capsize if we made an attempt to go ashore. And it absolutely poured with rain all day, non-stop.

At about nine in the evening the wind diminished and shifted direction and it stopped raining. I decided to row over for a beer in Boisdale's only pub.

On the walk up from the jetty I met a man in his fifties who had obviously had a few.

'Are you German?' he asked, without any niceties.

'No, Swedish.'

'No harm in that,' he said, raising a finger in greeting and ambling on. Because it was Saturday night, the pub was full – full of men, that is – all drinking assiduously standing up. South Uist is Catholic, like the other southern islands, and not as puritanical and orthodox as the Protestants

117

in the north (Catholics after all have the great advantage of being granted absolution for their sins if they sincerely repent; Balzac used to say that you couldn't write novels with Protestants as heroes because the story would end after their very first sin). On South Uist the tourists at least were allowed to do much as they liked on Sundays, fishing or walking, for instance. But having a drink of alcohol, even just a beer, was as forbidden here as further north. The Outer Hebrides are 'dry' on Sundays. The result is that people, which is to say men, drink enough to keep them going through the next day before the pub closes at eleven on Saturday night.

I had hardly got into the pub before a man about my own age came up to me and grabbed hold of my tartan scarf.

'Is that McKinley?' he asked, in a tone utterly devoid of any friendliness.

I explained who I was and that I had just happened to buy the scarf in a souvenir shop in Fort Augustus. Luckily I was believed and was actually bought a beer. I shudder to think what would have happened if I had belonged to the 'wrong' clan!

~

I was in Dunmore East on the south coast of Ireland. A thick milky fog had rolled in from the Atlantic an hour after I had moored. I sat in the cockpit congratulating myself on having arrived in time. Otherwise I would have had to spend the night at sea, and I was alone on board. I could scarcely make out the harbour entrance a hundred yards away, so it was to my great surprise that the prow of another yacht emerged out of the fog on its way in. It tied up alongside *Rustica*. At its stern was a flag unknown to me, black with a white cross. Later, in the bar of the yacht club, I got into conversation with the three elderly men from Wales who were sailing the boat and discovered that it was the 'Celtic' flag. When I asked why they were flying it, the skipper replied, 'It's the right thing to do when you sail to Ireland.'

~

Meetings like these are anecdotal, of course. But not solely. There seems to be something in Scotland, Ireland, Wales, Brittany and Galicia that still binds these stateless lands together; more than just the bagpipes which oddly enough are played in all the Celtic regions. What is the bond? The obvious answer is 'history', even if the traces of the original Celts in Galicia are slight and even though Galician is a Romance rather than a Celtic tongue. But what is a Celtic land? What distinguishes it from other countries? In modern times?

An analogy with the meanings of words may provide a partial answer. Many people seem to believe that words have an inflexible meaning, fixed for all time, which is the same as the original meaning. As 'evidence' of a word's meaning they point to its etymology, to its history. But meanings change. How otherwise would languages develop? How would Latin have become French, Spanish and Italian – to name just a few examples? The word 'romance', for instance, now primarily used to describe a relationship, previously a narrative in the vernacular language, is derived via the French from 'lingua romana' as opposed to 'lingua latina'. Most words have gone through changes of meaning.

And so it is with the character and culture of peoples. The fact that the Celtic lands today have a common Celtic history does not necessarily mean that what they have in common now is 'Celtic'. Their similarities could equally be based on something else, for instance that they have all suffered repression by other states or that they are all on the Atlantic seaboard.

We so-called educated Westerners should know how dangerous it is to generalise about a whole people's supposed mentality and characteristics. So let me first state my own fundamental rule quite categorically: we should always assume that a new and unknown person could be an exception to all rules. In other words, never pre-judge anyone.

But having said that, I still have a feeling from personal experience reinforced by reading, that there is a Celtic reality, vigour, energy or mood, which I tried to capture to some extent in *The Celtic Ring*.

Celtic music has undergone a significant resurgence in recent years. It has a lightness of spirit, a rhythm that seems to have throbbed for thousands of years; it is a primeval lament with a belief in life. Listen to Runrig's '*siol ghoridh/thairis air a ghleann*' to Karen Matheson's '*mi le m'uilinn*', to Barzaz' '*Al lezvamm*'! Once a year, in the town of Quimper in Brittany, an inter-Celtic music festival takes place. Hundreds of thousands of people make the pilgrimage to hear traditional Celtic music, whether it be Scottish, Irish, Welsh or Breton. The festival in 2000 drew a public of half a million! Thousands of Celtic musicians gather there to be inspired and learn from one another. A few years ago the Breton guitarist Dan Ar Braz had the idea of bringing together a hundred leading Celtic musicians and recording a CD. It became an unparalleled success, selling hundreds of thousands of copies and even inspiring a front-page article in *Le Monde* on the Celtic music phenomenon.

Is it in music that the Celtic soul is to be found nowadays?

In all the Celtic lands, and even beyond, there are Druid orders and Celtic associations with tens of thousands of members. Many of them are secret. Some, like the United Ancient Order of Druids in Sweden, with its five thousand members, probably have very little to do with genuine Celtic heritage. But others are as pagan as they are militant and claim to be descended from the original Druids, the Celts' mentors and intellectual leaders. Some of the orders stipulate at least one Celtic parent and the ability to speak a Celtic language as a prerequisite for admission to their exclusive membership.

Is it in these often secret orders that the original Celtic soul still flourishes?

There are independence parties in all the Celtic lands. The Scottish National Party, SNP, is the largest, but has achieved a bare thirty per cent in many elections. The Republic of Ireland doesn't need a nationalist party of course: all the major parties declare their adherence to Celtic traditions. In Northern Ireland there is Sinn Féin, whose slogan is 'Not only to be free, but also Celtic; not only to be Celtic, but also free'. Wales, Brittany and Galicia have their nationalist parties, which seldom manage to win any electoral seats, except on local councils. But they exist and keep themselves in the public eye.

Is it through politics and the nationalist parties that the remaining Celtic peoples are trying to reassert themselves?

In Wales there is an annual celebration, the Gorsedd, which is a kind of Celtic world championship in poetry. Poetry has high prestige in all the Celtic lands. The literature of Ireland is well enough known to need no special mention, but perhaps less familiar is the fact that all writers and artists with two or more works to their credit are exempt from Irish tax. The former Prime Minister Charles Haughey said he put forward the proposal in order to demonstrate that Ireland still held its bards in great esteem. In both Wales and Brittany there is a flourishing literature written and published in the Celtic languages. It survives against all the odds, and has had its own notable successes.

Is it in poetry and fiction that we should seek the quintessentially Celtic?

Go to Scotland, Ireland, Wales, Brittany, Galicia, even to Cornwall! Stand on the top of a cliff or on high ground with your nose pointed to the Atlantic in a howling westerly gale when the rain has given way to the ragged cumulus of a cold front scudding in over the land! You are standing on the western frontiers of Europe, on the edge of the unknown. It is easy to imagine, if you are so inclined, that *sid*, the paradise of the Celts, lies just over the horizon. The present regions with Celtic ancestry all have their faces turned towards the Atlantic. The Celts were pushed to the extreme west by the Romans, Anglo-Saxons and Germanic tribes. They held out along the 'Celtic fringe', on the brink of the abyss. What was it like for a people to stand with their backs to the ocean or to face it with bared chests and attempt to survive, with nowhere to turn? To be forced to survive against all the odds for more than a millennium at the end of the Earth must have left its mark.

Is that the invisible cement, a brew of suppression and exposure in a merciless but breathtakingly beautiful natural environment? Is the Celtic identity the result of having lived at the end of the Earth for over a thousand years?

~

I started writing my novel *The Celtic Ring* during my first winter in Dragør. It was not before time. After my youthful collection of short stories, *Splinters*, I actually wrote another novel, which foundered because of an immature skipper still wet behind the ears. There was nothing to salvage from the wreck, not even to make a modest fine-weather skiff for Sunday excursions on calm waters. A single gust of wind would have sent it to the bottom again.

It wasn't only the plot and material that were deficient. The whole vessel lacked course and character.

I had ideas for new novels in my head, but I didn't know what bearing to steer. One was to write 'something' about my cruises in Celtic waters and about Scotland. Another was to write a 'new' version of *The Riddle of the Sands*, that truly incomparable spy and sailing novel by Erskine Childers. A third was to write a book 'about' freedom (this last is always in my mind, of course).

But I could find neither structure nor direction.

Until one pitch-black January night in filthy weather when a catamaran came sailing into Dragør harbour with Pekka at the helm...

That is the tale I told in *The Celtic Ring*. The strangest aspect of that wintry and spooky apparition was probably not that a mad Finn was out sailing in mid-winter with 'a woman on board', but that I should be served an opening for a novel on a plate.

It took me no more than a few days to write the beginnings of a story whose end and resolution I had no idea of. I read *The Riddle of the Sands* for the umpteenth time, even though I knew it more or less by heart.

It is a remarkable book in many ways, if only because it has always stayed in print in one edition or another ever since it was first published in 1903. There are not many twentieth-century writers who can boast that, not even more significant authors than Childers. But the account of the sailing adventures of Carruthers and Davies around the East Frisian Islands, that blend of nautical description, espionage and characterisation, seems constantly to find a new audience.

Anyone who reads both *The Riddle of the Sands* and *The Celtic Ring* can certainly identify the borrowed plumage in which I dressed my own novel. One of my motives for writing *The Celtic Ring* was that I would have liked to read another novel by Childers myself.

The Celtic theme, on the other hand, was my own. Except that when Pekka sailed into Dragør that January evening I didn't know very much about the Celts and their history, and equally little about Childers as a person. All I knew about my then embryonic novel was that I was going to sail my yacht *Rustica* to Scotland and let her experience some frightening adventures.

My first idea was to let Torben and Ulf fall foul of the IRA or UFF, one of the two armed movements active in Northern Ireland, Catholic and Protestant respectively, who would stop at nothing. But it soon occurred to me that this was a serious matter of life and death, not a subject for a novel unless you really knew what you were talking about.

I had read a number of sizeable and credible books about Northern Ireland's murderous tragedy, but hardly enough to understand what it is that makes so many, in the name of God or ideology, think they have the right to kill others for a future which they cannot predict with any certainty.

So I set out on a different journey, into the realm of the Celts. I began to ponder the question of why I had felt so at home in Brittany and Scotland especially. I read a lot of books about Celtic history and discovered a world and a people whose existence I had hardly been aware of, the world I have already spoken of, here and elsewhere.

But I discovered too that it was not easy to find sources and documents. There was virtually nothing in Swedish. Even in English books were hard to obtain. A few individual titles in print, no more. My salvation lay in the fact that I know French, and in France I found what I needed, for example a doctoral thesis on current Druid lodges which gave an alarming perspective on something that to me had been no more than a curiosity.

Yet all in all the results were disappointing. The immediate cause is not hard to identify: according to Françoise Le Roux and Christian-J. Guyonvarc'h, authors of an excellent book on Druids based on Old Irish manuscripts, there are at most a score of academics in the world researching the history, culture, languages, architecture and literature of the Celtic regions.

No matter: I had what I needed to let fantasy merge with reality... and vice versa. I even imagined I was being fairly original. Who, in Sweden and maybe even in Europe, was writing a novel on Celtic prehistory and nationalism?

One imagines so much. It was about a year after I had begun my novel that a huge exhibition on the Celts opened its doors in Venice. Then came the music. Even old Donovan made a recording in Gaelic. Paddy Moloney, the piper in The Chieftains, said in an interview that twenty years earlier, when The Chieftains started playing traditional Irish music, there was only a handful of real pipers left in Ireland. Now there were several hundred, and most of them in his opinion damned good and very young. Newspapers, at least in France and Ireland, began to write about 'the Celtic revival'. I even have a CD in my collection with the evocative title *The Celts Rise Again*.

So the self-made myth of my own originality took a serious blow. But it was nothing compared with what was to come. My meetings, my experiences on the ground and the fruits of my reading had convinced me that it was quite possible that the Celtic lands would one day be independent; it was undoubtedly within the bounds of possibility – and thus of literature. So I imagined, on sound premises, that Brittany, Galicia, Scotland and Wales broke away from France, Spain and Britain. I saw in my mind's eye Britain being reduced to a medium-sized country in Europe, and the dream of the greatness of Great Britain and its Empire coming to an end once and for all.

I had hardly finished writing my novel before the Berlin Wall came tumbling down with a crash that shook the world. Not only that: it was immediately apparent that the great Soviet Empire had been no more than an ugly and tyrannical dream. New states came into being, old ones were resurrected.

What is there to say that my imaginary scenario might not be realised at any time? It is no more unbelievable or improbable than the tearing down of the Berlin Wall because people's suspicion and distrust of one another had reached such levels that not even a KGB general could rely on his orders being carried out.

As I write these lines even the situation in Northern Ireland has radically altered. The Good Friday Agreement between Ireland and Britain was the first step towards the integration of Ulster into Celtic Ireland. The referendum on increased home-rule for Scotland has taken place, with a large majority voting in favour of having their own parliament. A referendum in Wales produced a similar result, if not so clear-cut.

Rings on the water, then. We think ourselves original, perhaps especially as artists, but actually we are permeated by our times, by moods, ideas, forces and trends that are constantly but often indiscernibly flowing round the world.

The individualism and nationalism springing up like rampant weeds at the moment are but one example. And there is a paradox here, of course. Individualism, that strange phenomenon that believes that the individual has an existence independent of other people, that convinces itself that there is strength in isolation, is actually a collective ideology that has spread like wildfire in the West over the last few years. The ugly face of nationalism and the poison of racism likewise.

Although I took Erskine Childers' novel as my model and inspiration for *The Celtic Ring*, I didn't sit with it at my elbow and follow it slavishly in content and composition as I wrote. Ulf, Torben, MacDuff, Pekka and Mary had their own lives to lead, and I delved ever deeper into a Celtic history that had nothing to do with Prussia and the East Frisian Islands.

But the further west *Rustica* sailed, the closer came the tragic and brutal reality of present-day Northern Ireland: the irreconcilable war between the IRA and the UFF which has been going on for thirty years and has caused over three thousand deaths, three thousand living individuals who are gone for ever and who won't even know whether their deaths served any purpose, whether they were necessary to give others a slim chance of a better future.

I thus began to read more and more about what with unethical understatement are called 'the Troubles'. One of my prime sources of knowledge and insight was a book entitled *IRA* by Tim Pat Coogan, a well-known and respected journalist on *The Irish Times*. It was there, quite unexpectedly, that I again encountered Erskine Childers, in what was for me a wholly new guise: as one of the IRA's principal martyrs. He was shot by the first Irish government because he refused to recognise the agreement between Britain and Ireland under which the six predominantly Protestant counties of Ulster were to remain part of Great Britain. But that was not all. He had also smuggled weapons to the IRA during the war against Britain in his now legendary sailing yacht *Ansgar*. This aspect of Childers, I thought, could have been the prototype of my MacDuff. I had embodied Childers' vision in one of my own characters.

This discovery made a great impression on me. Whatever I thought, felt or imagined had already been thought, felt and lived.

Judging by the reactions in Sweden from critics and readers, the Celtic theme in my book was seen mainly as a sort of exotic décor, and could equally well have been something else, something neither deadly serious nor necessarily realistic.

When the book was published in France, however, reactions were totally different. At the University of Rennes, where I had been invited to speak, I had an audience of about a hundred and fifty, many of them from the Department of Celtic Studies. I was asked a number of fervent questions about identity, about French imperialism and repression, and about independence. Some of the questioners wanted me to take sides with the Celtic peoples. They wanted me to condemn centuries of repression and racism against Brittany, the Bretons and the Breton language.

But I was not prepared to allow myself to be used for purposes other than my own, any more than my book had been intended as an apologia.

In St-Malo I talked to the formerly Breton-speaking parents of a friend of mine. They had also read my book and declared themselves full of admiration for what I had achieved. What was that? In their opinion no less than making them realise that their own peaceful struggle for the

Breton language and culture was part of a much wider context, the pan-Celtic cause.

A few days later I gave a lecture at *Les Boréales*, an annual festival devoted to Scandinavian literature. A woman came up to me afterwards who had read my book and driven all the way from Le Havre just to hear my talk. She thanked me so warmly that I felt embarrassed. For what? For having made her understand, through my novel, why she had always felt an exile, living in Normandy, in France. I had made her realise that she was Breton first and everything else came second.

After I had finished my novel, *The Battle for Scotland* was published, written by Andrew Marr, a distinguished journalist on *The Economist*. His book confirmed with astounding precision many of my hypotheses and flights of fancy about ways in which the Scottish situation *could* develop. Even in 1992 Marr had been convinced that Scotland would become independent in the near future: 'And when it does speak, its voice will be sharp and fresh. And its views will perhaps surprise us.'

With the referendums that have already taken place there is every indication that Marr's predictions and my own in *The Celtic Ring* will come true. We will soon know whether Great Britain will be reduced to England, just a small country in northern Europe. I personally hope that this is what happens, irrespective of my partiality for Celtic culture. The smaller countries are, the less harm they can do if they go off the rails, even when they appropriate the ugly nationalism they had fought against to attain their independence.

Spreading rings on the water is the best way of improving the world.

~

What is the truth about the Celtic lands? I am only a sailor, amateur historian and novelist. I make no claim to have an answer to my own question. All I know for certain is that there is a need to seek an answer and that I intend to take part in the continuing search. That's all.

'*Everything is surely arranged to a different plan from the universally accepted one*,' Martinson writes in *Cape Farewell*, and demonstrates with as much clarity as he can muster that he as a true nomad distances himself from all nationalism: '*Eliminate all frontiers*'.

Yes, let's do it!

So that we can start to live.

On dreams and their fulfillment

Many people dream of a different kind of life altogether. It would be interesting but impossible to establish who and how many would rather live a life other than the one they are actually living. I am not referring to more money to buy a bigger car, a better stereo, a more powerful computer, expensive clothes, or to subscribe to more channels on satellite or cable TV. I am talking about freedom, or about money to buy yourself freedom.

It is an incontrovertible fact, I am sure, that you meet many dreamers among people who sail, especially men. Some are successful – they take to it like fish to water. Some are unsuccessful or hopeless cases – the ones who don't understand that they need their partner to transform their dreams into reality.

So what qualities are required to fulfil a dream? I would stress at least three: burning desire, persistence, and realism. This last is in my opinion the most essential. I know people who set themselves such lofty and fanciful goals that it is absolutely certain they will never attain them. There are even cases of dreams being deliberately formulated so as to remain out of reach. A safety precaution perhaps.

We are all quite within our rights to be the architects of our own happiness in our own way. If someone can find happiness by dreaming impossible dreams, dreams that will never be put into effect, there can surely be no objection. Though I have a shrewd suspicion that impossible dreams do not satisfy anyone, whether ordinary living people or fictional characters such as Flaubert's Emma Bovary or Cervantes' Don Quixote.

One of my earliest plans was to live for a year or so in Paris. It was a young man's dream, inspired by ambitions to be a writer, or at least to play at being one for a while. I had read Hemingway's *A Moveable Feast*, Orwell's *Down and Out in Paris and London*, Henry Miller's *Tropics*, the seven volumes of Anaïs Nin's diaries and four of Simone de Beauvoir's memoirs. Like these authors, I was going to sit in cafés and write. Not to become famous or a great writer as they did and as was their aim from the outset. I have never dared to be so pretentious. No, writing was – and still is – for me an attractive way of life, because it gives total freedom. I assumed. At the time I had no idea what demanding work it is to write a novel, or how infinitesimally few authors there are who can support themselves by their profession.

Anyway, the dream of 'living in Paris for a while and writing' was not particularly hard to implement. I worked for six months more or less round the clock to save money: delivered newspapers from four to six in the morning, took a temporary post as a schoolteacher from eight to three, and served in a bookshop on Friday afternoons and Saturdays. When the halfyear was up I had more than £2,000 in the bank and abnormally large calf muscles.

I bought a single ticket to Paris and got on a train. I had pre-arranged a month's grape-picking in the Beaujolais region to begin with. In the vineyards I met some Parisians of my own age, one of whom had relatives in Paris who rented out some *chambres de bonne*, those maid's rooms in the attic that are nowadays let to students, immigrants, or impoverished bohemian-artistic romantics like me. I was able to rent one of them, the simplest and cheapest, with washbasin, bed, table, chair and floral wallpaper – all for the very reasonable price of 120 francs a month. I moved in with my two suitcases and a correspondence course in French, lay down on the bed with some croissants and a newly-purchased paperback about the gentleman thief Arsène Lupin. I felt like a prince. I quickly calculated that my money would last for a year if I was careful, a whole year with no specific plans. If I had had a diary, every page would have been empty. It was life at its best. A blank page. An unstarted story.

The practical side of my dream had been put into effect, to my complete satisfaction.

On the other hand, the more idealistic side of the project was more elusive. I wrote, certainly, but I didn't feel like a writer. And I saw no sign whatsoever of the artistic melting-pot that Paris was reputed to be. It occurred to me eventually that the creative currents that had at various times flowed with such vitality through Paris had always been more or less invisible. Who knew Joyce, Hemingway, Miller, Anaïs Nin, Durrell, Beckett or Sartre at the time they were living their bohemian lives in Paris? Who could have foreseen that García Márquez would have turned out as he did when he sat in a freezing garret like mine keeping his neighbours awake tapping on his typewriter? When Existentialism was discovered by journalists and tourists it was not long before Sartre, Simone de Beauvoir, Camus and Genet were forced to leave the Café aux Deux Magots because of all the inquisitive and intrusive autograph hunters. The nearest I came to meeting a writer was probably the day I was approached by a homosexual poet who claimed to be writing a novel about a minibus-load of French poets on their way through Sweden to the Arctic Circle. I was – unfortunately – the first Swedish writer he had ever encountered. So he wanted me as an object of study – at far too close quarters.

Besides, my more romantic dreams of becoming a writer had taken a buffeting the previous year, when I had stayed in a little hotel near Notre-Dame for two months. As soon as I moved into my miserable but cheap room I went into town, bought a pen and notebook, settled myself in a café and ordered an espresso to last me several hours while my pen flew over the paper. If I remember correctly I was writing a crime novel set in Jönköping, my home town. The name of the protagonist was Jillis, a jeweller and amateur detective, living in a former turpentine factory that he had converted himself. Not bad, eh? Anyway, I was busily writing and rewriting. But after an hour had passed, *le garçon*, the waiter, was suddenly standing in front of me with a severe expression on his face.

'*Monsieur*,' he said curtly, '*il faut consommer!*'

Which roughly translated meant, 'Are you ready to order something else, Sir?' Or, interpreted more fully, he was telling me that if I couldn't afford at least an espresso an hour, I should get the hell out of his café.

What about Sartre? I thought to myself. How did he manage to spend the whole day over his tepid coffee writing for all he was worth?

It was only later that it dawned on me that I had made my attempt at playing the writer in one of the large well-frequented tourist cafés around Notre-Dame, the kind that no Parisian would ever set foot in. It was hardly the place for me to realise my dream of living the bohemian and creative literary life I had read about in books.

Even today Paris is a magnet for writers. There are many Swedish authors, both young and old, who have felt the urge to spend a period of apprenticeship in the capital of France. I don't know what dreams and experiences they had, but I know it is extremely unrealistic to go to a city with a population of ten million in the hope of bumping into and befriending the artists who will be the Bretons, Sartres, Hemingways or Becketts of tomorrow.

I read an interview with Nathalie Sarraute in *Le Monde* once in which she said she still, at her advanced age (then 88!) spent several hours every morning in a café writing. But, she added with a certain relish, no one in her café knew of the fame concealed behind the wrinkles and grey hair. Nor of course did she divulge which café she patronised.

And that is how it mostly is. Any famous authors worth their salt want to be left to write in peace. And the great writers-to-be are lost in the crowd.

So, realism is the vital ingredient for anyone wanting to fulfil a dream and to minimise the disappointment when reality turns out to be exactly as a little imagination and insight could have predicted.

~

In our first winter on board *Rustica*, Helle and I sat in the cabin one evening checking our finances.

At that point we had owned the boat for a year. Of the £10,000 she had cost, in fairly shabby condition but otherwise sound, except for the engine, we had paid off £7,000, and invested a great deal of money in making her winterproof: insulation, oilstove, new vents, seven coats of epoxy resin paint on the hull since we were going to be in the water all year round, a new hatch in the forepeak instead of the old leaky one, condensation-absorbing paint against the damp. We had also had the engine serviced, the mainsail repaired after it tore in our first summer, and a new diesel tank installed when holes had suddenly appeared in the existing galvanised one.

It was all a considerable financial outlay for us, not being well off and with only a modest income. Helle had just finished her studies and was looking for a job. I had a part-time post as a French teacher at a vocational college for the unemployed. Our resources were totally disproportionate to the scope of our dreams: paying off the boat, equipping her for long voyages and then sailing for a couple of years at liberty without a thought for the morrow.

That dark winter evening, lubricated by a good dinner and an equally good bottle of red wine, we had decided it was time to plan our finances in more detail. It was not that difficult. The balance of the loan for the boat had to be paid off. Then there was the equipment still needed to get *Rustica* ready to take us safely out on the high seas. Longdistance sailors will recognise the list: life-raft, emergency flares, dinghy, wind vane, autopilot, VHF radio, satellite navigation system, spares for the engine, anchor chain, plough anchor and capstan, storm jib, radar reflector, mast steps, lifelines on deck, charts and pilot books. But since *Rustica* was an elderly lady we would also attire her in a new set of cruising sails and she would have a sprayhood, new batteries, new echo sounder, new tiller and a whole lot more. We estimated the overall cost of equipment to be £13,000. To sail for two years we reckoned on £17,000, including such unforeseeable eventualities as engine failure, repairs and tickets home. As we finished the bottle of wine, we totalled up. The tidy sum we needed to save was £35,000! That was after tax. And we had to live while we saved. Preferably not too poorly. Preferably not so frugally that we couldn't drink a bottle of wine with our meals occasionally and buy one of those indispensable and re-readable books that we had no space for. All in all it was going to cost over £40,000 after tax to fulfil our otherwise perfectly feasible and pragmatic dream!

When we had finished our calculations Helle looked at me and said in a tone of resignation, 'We'll never do it!'

Yet five years later the boat was paid for and fully equipped. We had £12,000 in the bank and could afford to buy a few crates of beer for a leave-taking from our friends in Langelinie harbour in Copenhagen. How was it possible?

In our case it was living on board the boat that did the trick. We were able to keep our outgoings down rather than increasing our income. Just think: a winter berth for six months in a normal harbour seldom costs more than £150. Heating expenses are minimal. No TV licence, no phone bills, no newspapers, no car, our only insurance was for the boat, and so forth. On average I would say that our fixed monthly outlay, excluding food, was around £80 per person. For ordinary people the best way to save money is not by stressing themselves out to earn more, but by reducing outgoings; in other words, by lowering consumption.

～

In Falmouth I met two Swedes on their way home in an Omega 30. They had been in the Caribbean, like so many dreamers among sailors, and had one month remaining of their sabbatical year and leave of absence. I asked them whether it had been worth the trouble and the tens of thousands it must have cost them to equip their boat and live with no income for a year.

'Yes,' they replied with one voice, 'but we would never do it again.'

To fulfil their dream within a year they had had to spend almost half that time at sea. Which is an indication of just how far it is to the Caribbean. Is it necessary to sail so far, when your time is limited? I am convinced many people would still give themselves lifelong memories if they restricted their aspirations to nearer horizons. Or at least if they weren't so fixated on sun, warmth, palm trees and coral reefs. It is a sad fact that very few people sail to the Caribbean to get to know the local people and their culture. Their curiosity often stretches no further than tasting the rum. And then these long-distance sailors come home complaining about their reception, that the locals were only after their money.

My own present dream has the working title 'Stornoway'. It is seductively simple: to spend a year on board *Rustica* in the Outer Hebrides, overwintering in the town of Stornoway on the island of Harris. But it could equally well be something else, a year on the canals of France, a winter in an empty harbour in Poland or on Corsica, six months from April to November in a largely deserted natural harbour on the west coast of Sweden or southern Norway. The possibilities for an undemanding and realistic, but imaginative, dreamer are almost infinite.

Lovers of order will wonder as always how anyone can dream of spending a long, dark, windy winter in the Outer Hebrides. What is there to do or see there?

The answer is as seductively simple as the dream: I don't know – or: we shall see – or: people, sea and sky.

> Nothing is worse than when the matter-of-factness of the world
> penetrates into the worlds of your dreams with its drab monotony.
>
> (*Aimless Travels*)

No, what is the point of a dream which is *only* reality?

On maps, charts and pilot books

I had a dream of one day sailing to Madagascar. Maybe I still have. Some years ago when I was in Weilbach's, the principal chart shop in Copenhagen, it occurred to me to ask what charts they had beyond Europe.

'What would you like?' came the response.

'What have you got?' I asked.

'The whole world.'

The whole world instantly available on demand! The whole world in stock!

Probably only someone who sails and dreams of sailing long-distance can understand the yearning such an answer inspires. Though there might have been a hint of a smile on the sales assistant's face. I can't have been the first dreamer to have bought a piece of the world over the counter.

'Could I have a chart of Madagascar?' I asked.

'Certainly,' the assistant replied, as if nothing could be more natural.

I had to indicate which chart I required in the British Admiralty Catalogue. I selected one of the entire island, from north to south, east to west.

It was an excited dreamer who left the shop with Madagascar under his arm.

Only when I unrolled it on the table in the cabin did I realise what sort of chart I had spent so much money on. Madagascar is roughly twice the size of Sweden, and this covered the whole island and even part of the coast of Africa! My purchase, the stuff of dreams in waiting, was actually a small-scale chart, the kind you would use to find Madagascar – or to sail safely past it, which is the usual course. But if nothing else, it gave me an idea of the immense size of the island.

A few weeks later, having sensed my disappointment, Helle went to Weilbach's and bought me another chart, this time just of the northern tip of the island. And there you could pick out the coral reefs and all the little bays where the pirates of old had once hidden from the authorities and the punitive expeditions that were despatched to hunt them down.

I take out this chart from time to time and run my eye over the northern coastline on imaginary voyages. Trying to picture the scene in these anchorages, I read off the contour lines along the coast to see how much lee it would provide and note that there are symbols for mangroves, the trees whose roots are so deep that they make excellent mooring points in hurricanes.

There is no doubt that charts are the yachting dreamer's prime tool. But they would serve poets and artists equally well.

However, it needs long experience, serious training and a generous ration of scepticism to use them as a basis for acquainting yourself with reality. All competent navigators know that errors are legion and that reality can come up with many a surprise.

～

In recent times a number of thinkers, among them some self-styled philosophers, have advocated the theory that we human beings are fundamentally incapable of communicating with one another, that a linguistic message is always equivocal, subjective, open to interpretation. Some argue that each of us goes around with his private picture of reality in his head, different from everyone else's, that each person is as unique as his fingerprints, and that it is a fundamental principle that we cannot know the nature of reality. Even if we could know, we would not be able to convey that same knowledge to anyone else. These philosophers maintain that both knowledge and communication are subjective and relative. In other words, that man is an island. Or, as Simone de Beauvoir said, that all we can know for certain is that the only thing which unites us as human beings is our isolation.

Ideas such as these, however absurd they may seem to the average man or woman of sound mind, are not new. They have been promulgated and defended ever since Plato happened to enter a cave with his back to the entrance, without explaining how he got there or that he could turn and look out of it instead of at the wall. This same turning-yourback philosophy thrives today under names like deconstructivism, postmodernism or epistemological scepticism and relativism. The major proponents are Lyotard, Derrida, Foucault, Paul de Man, Rorty, Quine and many acolytes of lesser stature.

To my doubtless naïve mind it is easy to demonstrate the absurdity of many of these theories. If the assertion, 'All linguistic meaning is subjective, relative and private', or any variant of it, were true, it would also apply to the semantic significance of the assertion itself. Its own asserted meaning is negated by its own truth.

But you don't need to seek out such abstract arguments. In questions like these we can refer to the inexorable demands made at sea, where it can sometimes, ironically enough, feel like having firm ground beneath your feet.

The Clyde Cruising Club in Scotland publishes a series of handbooks on sailing in the Hebrides. Corryvreckan is a strait of ill repute between the islands of Jura and Scarba where the tidal stream runs at up to ten knots, and since it is narrow, the difference in level can be as much as one and a half metres from one end to the other. That means you would have to sail either uphill or downhill if you ventured in. But before taking such a rash step you would be well advised to read the Clyde Cruising Club's *Sailing Directions and Anchorages*:

> It is at its most dangerous when an Atlantic swell, having built up after several days of strong w{esterly} winds, meets a flood tide. A passage at this time would be unthinkable. {...} The overfalls close to the 29m sounding are invariably the most awesome, on occasion with breaking

crests and spume at their tops. In calm weather at sp{ring tides} the first can rise to a height of 4m, and may be accompanied by a loud, roaring noise as it plunges from the Scarba shelf. A heavy w{esterly} swell can double its height, when it and the remaining overfalls drop to the bottom of the deep, and possibly angled, troughs. In extreme conditions the roar can continue for several hours, audible even at Crinan, miles distant. {...} Prolonged strong w{esterly} winds can make an overfall, perhaps better described as a solid wall of water, stretch from here, and also from the shelf, right across the gulf {of Corryvreckan}.

Note particularly that the four-metre-high tidal seas are in *calm* weather. And the word 'possibly' applied to troughs is thought-provoking in itself. It obviously means that no one has ever been able to check at close quarters.

Now some philosophers state that every linguistic utterance can be interpreted to mean more or less anything – for example, in the case of Corryvreckan, that the tidal waters are not at all as dangerous as the text seems to imply. I don't know whether deconstructivists practise any sports other than 'going out for a cycle ride', but if they were yachtsmen there would be a very simple way of putting their own theories to the test: to ignore all the written or spoken warnings and to sail through Corryvreckan, from east to west, with the tidal current and against a south-west gale, force eight.

Unfortunately there is one major drawback to this experiment: we couldn't be sure that the sailing relativist would ever be in a position to say who was right – the one who took the warning at its word or the one who interpreted it in his own mind (quite apart from the fact that we couldn't rely on understanding the relativist's report even if, against all expectations, he survived).

I am not arguing that it is always easy to communicate or to know what is reality. On the contrary, it often demands much effort and good will to agree on what words actually mean. That is why we need science, because our cognisance of reality is not straightforward and unmediated.

But to be fair and undogmatic let us also give an example of the need for careful attention, experience and training to interpret charts and pilot books correctly.

After Torben had left *Rustica* and me in the last of the summer sun, I still had a month ahead of me on my own in Kinsale and on the yacht. I was looking forward to being alone because it focuses your attention in a way that is never possible when you are with others. The one disconcerting factor was that *Rustica* was moored beyond the outermost pontoon jetty in Kinsale marina with over a nautical mile of open water to the east. In the summer, when the risk of gales and storms is negligible, even in Ireland, and particularly from the east, there would have been nothing to worry about. But it was autumn now and low pressure systems were starting to appear over the mountains to the west. Giles, the harbourmaster, had told me I couldn't have a place inside the marina until November at the earliest. So I had to resign myself to listening to the weather forecasts just as much as if I were out sailing or lying at anchor in some godforsaken spot with no lee at any point of the compass.

One day, at noon, as I had feared, the Irish meteorological office issued an easterly gale warning. And of course, as always seems to be the case, even though in fact it isn't, the storm would hit us in the evening and continue through the night.

I went over to see John on the steel-hulled *Abba,* which was also moored outside, to share the bad news. He looked at me in disbelief.

'It's not what the weather fax showed this morning,' he said. 'But come aboard and we'll get a new synopsis.'

The weather fax is a wonderful machine from which you can obtain printed weather maps of large parts of the world, with isobars, millibars and everything you require to make your own forecasts of the progress of low pressure systems. John tapped a few buttons and a weather map of the Atlantic gradually emerged. And true enough, a few hundred nautical miles west of the cliffs of Ireland was an alarming area of low pressure of 950 millibars in the centre of dense isobar lines, a sure sign of fierce winds.

'But look at this!' said John, picking up the faxed map of that same morning. 'The depression is moving north-east and will pass north of Ireland. Exactly as usual. There'll be a storm, all right, but from the west, so we'll be okay.'

At eight in the evening, in an ominous dirty-yellow dusk, the wind arrived. An hour later, in pitch darkness and driving rain, it had reached gale force.

And it was easterly.

The next six hours until three o'clock in the morning can only be described as hellish. The waves that hit *Rustica*'s port side and cascaded over the deck in a never-ending stream must have been a metre high, the same height as the boat's freeboard. The combined fury of wind and waves transformed eight-inch-thick fenders into what looked like rubber planks, and one of them burst without my even noticing it in the thunderous noise.

I mostly lay on my bunk, dressed in full oilskins and boots, listening to the radio and smoking and drinking coffee. Every once in a while I climbed up on to the jetty, checked the mooring ropes and pushed the fenders down as best I could, since they had a tendency to ride up.

When it was at its very worst I actually packed a case with the most important items, money, passport, credit cards, manuscript of my novel *Long John Silver*, the GPS-navigator, some other expensive electronic equipment and a few irreplaceable books. My life was never at risk, at least as long as I kept my balance on the wildly leaping pontoon jetties, but *Rustica*'s survival was certainly in jeopardy. All that was needed was for the fenders to give way under the pressure.

But they held, and at about three o'clock the wind suddenly slewed round to the north-east, without slackening, where the land lay just a few hundred metres away. Ten minutes later the waves had subsided, everything returned to relative calm and I sank into a deep slumber, only to wake at ten with a stiff neck, still in my oilskins and boots. Seldom has breakfast tasted so good as it did that morning. The hastily packed suitcase and the burst fender remained as tangible signs of how close we had come to the danger mark. Quite a few boats sustained damage that night, even ones within the protection of the outermost jetty.

I wondered afterwards how *Rustica* had survived the brutal offensive at all. The answer must be twofold. Firstly, we were tied up to a pontoon jetty which was bouncing up and down in the swell at exactly the same tempo as the boat, without creating a backwash. The fact that both boat and jetty moved must have taken the sting out of the waves' anger. I wouldn't want to repeat the experiment to find out, but I'm almost certain that *Rustica* would soon have been a complete wreck if she had been moored at a stone or concrete jetty in similar circumstances.

Secondly, I think the tidal current, which runs at a couple of knots in the River Bandon, had a damping effect on the waves. The current was running across the wind direction when it was blowing at its hardest. It certainly felt as if the waves ought to have been even bigger and heavier and more powerful than they were.

So you could say that *Rustica* and I were fortunate in adversity.

When I met John in the morning he was profuse in his apologies. He and I both knew that the false judgement could have cost my boat her life, even if not that of his own *Abba*, a strongly-built steel forty-footer.

So what had happened? Quite simply, in all its incomprehensible complexity, the depression had changed course. Instead of racing on to the northeast it had suddenly shot into the Bay of Biscay. And we, then north of the centre of low pressure, got an easterly storm.

There you are, the relativist and doubter of objective knowledge would triumphantly cry. You can never know the real nature of reality. Everything is a matter of subjective interpretation, or even of personal opinion.

But that method of reasoning can lead to erroneous and irresponsible conclusions. There was nothing wrong with John's and my mutual understanding. We understood each other perfectly, even though we were both wrong. I interpreted the lines on the fax in exactly the same way as he did. Our error was not one of interpretation. We interpreted the maps correctly from the information we had to hand. What didn't occur to us was that the Irish weather forecast was based on later and thus more up-to-date information than our print-outs. So it wasn't a matter of interpreting reality, but rather a question of who to rely on when you don't have all the relevant information: yourself or the experts. In this case we should have relied on the experts, with their many weather stations and mega-computers.

Finally, if deconstructivists want to maintain that the storm and my experience of it are just a half-baked sailor's yarn, I have to conclude that they are crazy and need locking up. What else should I believe?

Only a fool, by the way, would even think of sailing through the whirlpools and tidal race of Corryvreckan in winds stronger than a gentle caress. But there are plenty of fools about.

Leaders, where are you taking us? Do you know what you are doing, or do we lie at the mercy of your restless and splenetic ambitions, your sick souls? Have you charted the world, mountains and seas; the countries of delusion and the rivers of hypothesis? Do you reckon with the creeping undergrowth of desire through the jungle of mankind? Have you ears to hear the stammering attempts at speech of deaf and dumb spirits and the barbarians who dwell outside the regions of form, colour and word?

We know that you desire much and that you believe much. But what do you know? What can you do?

You are well-dressed and your manner is restrained. Your armadas, your proud ships obey you maybe for a dozen years; then comes your decline and fall. Then we shall have to clear up after you and build bridges. Simplehearted, efficient technicians ruled by subtle schemers after power is the fashion today, but again and again Man steps forward with human desires and human soul, above and beyond the crises of stale mass-government.

For human beings remain throughout the first and the last.

(*Cape Farewell*)

On dragging anchor and sitting on watch

Lying at anchor in a breathlessly beautiful bay, with gulls and snorting seals our only company, is for me and a few others as close to paradise as we can get. But everyone who sails knows that a deserted paradise can be transformed into a purgatory in a matter of hours. The fear of dragging anchor in the middle of the night when the wind gets up and changes direction can lead to endless nights on watch sitting fully clothed and equipped endeavouring to take a bearing from indistinct contours ashore.

We met a Finnish couple in Limhamn harbour near Malmö on their way home after having spent three years in the Mediterranean and Caribbean. We discussed anchoring, as one does: thickness of chain, types of anchor and so forth. He was totally laid back about it, but she had never really been able to relax when they swung at anchor far from the beaten track with only themselves to rely on.

She had found a remedy, however: she would tie a piece of string to the anchor chain, passing it through the open forepeak hatch and twisting the other end round her finger. If the wind rose and tautened the anchor chain, her hand would lift and she would wake up. He said that sometimes when he woke in the night he could see her arm rising and falling like a pump handle without her even being aware of it. Her response was that it was only powerful tugs that woke her. And she was delighted with her system.

I am probably somewhere between the two extremes myself.

We left Kinsale on the first of April after our overwintering, in glorious weather, the first spring-like day. The wind was light and the sun glistened on the sea.

The next day brought a force eight gale, forty-five miles an hour, and rain. And so it continued more or less the whole month we tried to sail the south-west coast of Ireland. Deep depressions, dark and heavy with rain, swept in from the Atlantic every other day while we lay low in one anchorage after another. It was exhausting.

After two uncomfortable days in Glandore with westerly winds we had a one-day respite before the next storm hit us, this time with south-easterly winds as forecast, which made Glandore an impossible haven. We weighed anchor and sailed round to Castletownshend.

This is a remarkable place, consisting of not much more than a castle, a quay that is dry at low tide and a single street that vanishes up into heaven. It is so steep, lined with grey stone houses built on the slant, that all the cars are parked with their front wheels turned in to the kerb. It is said that the inhabitants develop a special gait from walking up and down their own village street, from the harbour at the bottom to the post office at the top. And indeed we several times saw the evidence for ourselves as we watched elderly ladies shuffling up the steep hill bent almost double.

This was my second visit and we anchored in the same spot as the year before, a cable-length off the quay, with due regard for the three-metre difference between high and low tide. The anchor bit first time when we put the engine full astern.

Backing the anchor in is also something we learnt from sailing in exposed waters. In Scandinavia you often see people letting out the anchor rope and casually laying the table for lunch before the anchor has even touched bottom.

But in British waters anchoring is a complicated procedure. For a start, almost everyone has a chain. It's no coincidence that nearly all boats that drag their anchor when the wind is howling and continually shifting only have rope. And you only see anchors of tried and tested brands: Bruce, CQR, Delta, Danforth and now Fortress. Imitations wouldn't be worth the bother. Nor would lead plates or umbrella anchors. And it is essential to ensure the anchor really has got a grip. Hence full astern and exact bearings to check that the boat is lying steady. If the anchor doesn't hold against a normal diesel engine on full speed astern, it won't hold the boat in a gale.

Perfectionists also leave the key in the ignition and have the halyard attached to the mainsail all the time they're riding at anchor. No question of putting the boom cover on for anyone who really knows his stuff. The chain has to be made fast below deck with a short strong piece of rope that can easily be sliced through with a knife if you can't free the anchor when you have to make a quick getaway. Finally, before anchoring can be regarded as complete, you plot a course on the chart that will get you out of the anchorage, and set the satellite navigator and echo sounder to anchor watch.

Only when all that is done can there be any hope of enjoying the peace of lying at anchor. But whatever preparations and safety measures you take, there is still no guarantee that you will keep your composure when it blows up in earnest.

When we anchored in Castletownshend on that day of respite between the two deep low pressure systems, the sun was shining and the wind gentle. Yet by evening the same day it was blowing from west-southwest at forty-five miles an hour. Helle and I went in and lay down, but I couldn't fall asleep and just lay listening to the groaning of the chain in the hawse. Finally I had to get up, put on my warm clothes, oilskin trousers, boots, and sit at the chart table, where I lit a candle and a cigarette, poured myself a cup of coffee and sat staring out of the window to check our bearings by the lights ashore. It was virtually hopeless. The gusts were changing direction all the time so that *Rustica* was swinging through ninety degrees. I went up on deck periodically and stood at the bow, looked at the heavy chain as taut as a wire and tried to take new bearings. I put my ear to the chain to listen for the special rattling that would mean we were dragging: the sound of the anchor scraping along the sea-bed.

I was bleary-eyed and exhausted by morning. At first light I could see we hadn't moved an inch and I realised the anchor would hold against worse than this. By that stage it must have dug itself a metre or more into the clay. I went back to the cabin and slept like a top.

Later that day the sun came out again, shining with a harsh brightness, and the wind veered to the north-west and increased to storm force. Helle and I rowed ashore with some difficulty and went for a walk beside the turbulent sea. When we came back we could see *Rustica* lurching from side to side. The anchor was holding for now, but what would happen if the wind rose even more? We decided to seek safer shelter. Further into the bay, round a point, there seemed to be sufficient space for one boat, if the depth were adequate. It was obviously not by chance that Castle-townshend's own few fishing boats were moored to buoys just behind that point. We weighed anchor and motored in. We tried four times to make the anchor grip, but without success. In the end we borrowed a vacant buoy in the hope that it didn't have an owner for the time being. We stayed on that buoy for a week while the depression and gale-force winds continued to sweep in over southern Ireland. But what happened when the series of low pressure systems abated and was followed by an eagerly anticipated band of high pressure? It parked itself right where we were, with close-packed isobars, and blew a northerly gale for another twenty-four hours. Despite the high pressure. Talk about bad luck!

When this also finally abated we sped off to Baltimore, where we were to visit Dermot and Diana Kennedy, whom we had met the previous year. We anchored in the roads outside the harbour, once again in bright sunshine and light wind.

The respite lasted a day. The weather forecast in the evening announced a south-easterly gale of forty miles an hour. We couldn't believe our ears. The only cheering factor was that we were nicely in the lee for a south-easterly. But two days later the wind sheered round to the west and we suddenly had more than a nautical mile of open water stretching in front of our prow. Dermot came out in his dinghy and offered us the loan of his buoy behind a point a little further along. We accepted with gratitude, because we had already started to drag.

We then spent another week on Dermot's buoy in fierce gales and driving rain. It blew so hard one day that we couldn't get ashore at all. Not because the waves were too big, but because we couldn't row our inflatable against the wind. But even on other days it was rather hazardous to go ashore or back out to *Rustica*. With the wind astern the inflatable flew over the water and we had to aim accurately or else risk being blown past the yacht and then having to spend hours battling back against the wind.

It is debilitating to have such powerful winds constantly in your ears, even if you're safely moored. And it was unsettling that we were standing on the bottom for an hour at low tide several days running. We had arrived in Baltimore just when the variation between high and low tide was at its maximum. The water wasn't quite enough for *Rustica*'s draught.

Some people wonder how you pass the time on days like those. You read good books, you chat, even if not much, cook meals and eat, listen to the radio, either exotic foreign tongues if possible, or music, carry out odd jobs on the boat, read up on your next destination, plan your route on the chart and mark in courses and distances, sit in the cockpit and gaze at sky, sea and nature, drink a bottle of wine in the evening. I myself also polish stones and write books. If you have all you need on board, then for me at least it is no deprivation to be unable to go ashore for a few days. The only thing that can wear on your nerves is the wind, when it is never silent, not even for a second. But provided it doesn't go on too long, you can put up with it, and even become so accustomed to it that you can almost hear the proverbial pin drop while the gale whistles around you.

> Travelling is not living with laughter in Tuscany or learning the art of juggling with three oranges in sunny Sicily. Travelling can be inching one's way round the world in pain and torment.
>
> (*Aimless Travels*)

On casting off

Countless books have been published about casting off, in both a literal and a metaphorical sense. It might be assumed that the former must be simple in comparison with the difficulties of severing one's bonds to life and people ashore. There can surely be no special knack in casting off the end of a rope.

Yet it is often just that, a knack, to put out from a quay in an onshore wind or reverse out from a pontoon jetty when the tidal current is running at a couple of knots across the marina. In Tréguier, for instance, it is almost impossible to tie up or cast off other than at the turn of the tide if you haven't been brought up with tidal streams and know how to sail obliquely between the jetties. Though the practical difficulties of casting off should never be exaggerated: there is always the option of waiting till the wind turns or the current slackens.

Procrastinating with the decision to cast off your moorings in the metaphorical sense is far worse. Some people spend half their lives planning their dream trip without getting away. There are even those who prefer planning to actual travelling. And why not? There is no doubt that a journey in the imagination can give great satisfaction. And it is significantly cheaper.

On the other hand, you cannot be entirely sure that even a fantasy journey is absolutely safe and sound. Madness can lie in wait at journey's end if you travel too long and too far.

There are plenty of clichés, all too many. You meet them everywhere, tired hackneyed refrains that hinder clear thought and distort the emotions. For what prompts most emotional attitudes? What you *think* of as reality, including your own inner reality. It is only those who see ghosts who are afraid of them. Only those who believe in God have cause to fear him. Only those who imagine that people are fundamentally evil and egotistical or Freudian sexual deviants treat their fellow human beings accordingly.

One of those worn-out expressions is 'planning the journey is half the fun'. If this were true, you could just plan two trips in a row and then stay at home. No, planning a journey can be a pleasure and a superlative stimulus for the imagination. Or it can be a nightmare. All depending on the circumstances.

Casting off your moorings in the metaphorical sense can be an incomparable relief. But it can also involve a heart-rending separation from your anxious nearest and dearest. Cutting the umbilical cord is for some the embodiment of freedom, for others insecurity incarnate.

Parting has always been a fundamental aspect of the human condition. In Jungian terms we could say that parting, in all its shades and forms, is an archetypal human experience. Nobody can live through a whole life without cutting adrift, even if it is not until the death of parents.

I am an omnivore as far as literature is concerned. Two of my favourite books are Chrétien de Troyes' *Perceval, ou le Conte du Graal* and *As I Walked Out One Midsummer Morning* by Laurie Lee. More than seven hundred years divide the two: how could they have anything in common? Chrétien's book, written around 1180, tells of Perceval's and Gawain's quest for the Holy Grail. We are at the court of King Arthur, miracles abound, beautiful princesses and fantastic adventures come flooding forth as from a never-ending magic spring. Laurie Lee's book seems to be totally different. It is the story of a young Englishman, Laurie Lee himself, setting out to see the world, with his violin as his only company. He leaves home on foot, takes a boat to Spain, and plays for his board and lodging on his wanderings, ignorant of the events and evils of the world, until the Spanish Civil War catches up with him and he is sent home to a country that soon no one can leave except for war and death, rather than for the enhanced life that Laurie Lee had envisaged.

What could be further apart than these two stories? One about noble knights seeking the elusive and mystical Grail, the other about a young man's walk through Spain in the twentieth century.

You don't need to read many pages to find at least one similarity: the son's farewell to his mother.

His mother, who loved him dearly, embraced him. 'My handsome son, my handsome son, may God protect you and always lead you in His ways. May He grant you more joy than I now have.' When the boy had gone a stone's throw he looked back and saw his mother lying in a faint at the end of the bridge. He gave his horse a flick of the whip on the rump and, to prevent himself returning, departed at speed into the great dark forest.

～

The stooping figure of my mother, waist-deep in the grass and caught there like a piece of sheep's wool, was the last I saw of my country home as I left it to discover the world. She stood old and bent at the top of the bank, silently watching me go, one gnarled red hand raised in farewell and blessing, not questioning why I went. At the bend of the road I looked back again and saw the gold light die behind her; then I turned the corner, passed the village school and closed that part of my life for ever.

Two young men set off on a journey and leave their mothers and a whole way of life behind them, perhaps never to return. Why are they going? What is it that makes them leave what they hold most dear, at the risk of losing it for ever?

When I read these two extracts I have a distinct sense of *déjà vu*, of seeing an event, full of nostalgia and sorrow, that has been repeated thousands of times throughout history.

When my mind turns to all the wars that are constantly taking place on our Earth, I often think of leave-taking, mothers and fathers, wives, daughters and sons, sweethearts and lovers seeing their young man off to war. How is it possible for them to let him go? I think too of the millions of emigrants in the course of history, of all those who are now called immigrants and despised and mocked as much as emigrants were once admired and respected for their energy and belief in the future.

And I think sometimes of myself. When I was seven years old my father drowned in a boating accident in a lake in Västmanland in central Sweden, with six other adults and two boys. The lake was called Nedre Vettern. My maternal grandfather, whom I never knew, also drowned in a boating accident, in a lake near the southern end of Lake Vättern and Jönköping.

Nevertheless I have devoted my life to river and lake and sea. I started as a skin diver, became an instructor and then went on to sail. I purchased my first boat at the age of twenty-two, long before *Skum*, for fifty pounds. It was a West Coast skiff that was laid up on a river near Kåseberga, east of Ystad on the south coast of the province of Skåne. The best that could be said of that boat was that the hull was watertight. I bought a pair of oars and decided to row it round to Malmö. Wearing a wetsuit as my only safety equipment, I set out on a warm spring day and rowed straight across Ystad Bay. I was only a few miles offshore and crossing the route of the ferries to Germany and Poland out of Ystad harbour. The weather was calm and I reached Abbekås, about twenty miles across the bay, late in the evening, pulled the boat up on the beach and slept there in a sleeping bag. The next day the wind had sprung up from the west and the waves were a metre high. I put out, but got nowhere in the headsea and turned back after a couple of hours, beached the boat and took the bus back to Lund.

Today I am astounded at my reckless folly. If it had blown up from the north when I was out in the middle of the bay, I would never have reached land again. And I had not even listened to the weather forecast!

So I have a mother whose father and husband both drowned and a sister whose father and grandfather drowned. Yet off I go without for a moment trying to understand how they must feel when I put out from Thyborøn in an IF-boat to cross the North Sea, or when I say I am thinking of being away for a few years at sea on *Rustica*. If I think of it at all it's tactical, for example not phoning my mother to say we intend to sail the next day, because I imagine it is easier for her to control her anxiety if she can persuade herself that I am not out on the North Sea when the weather forecast (which she always listens to) reports gales off the west coast of Denmark.

The thought of not setting out doesn't occur to me. I, like so many before me, like Perceval and Laurie Lee, like hundreds of thousands of others, left without looking back. Why? What is it that drives us, sailors or not? I don't know. What I do know is that for me it is a question of life, not of death. I have no thought at all of flirting with death, no thought of taking revenge by conquering the water that killed my father and grandfather, no thought of causing anguish to my loved ones.

My father had an older friend, Vilhelm Norström, who after my father's death treated me, young as I was, as if I were grown up and as if I too were his friend. He worked for the council, digging ditches, and belonged to a category later known as 'working class educational potential', without ever having the chance to turn that potential into a better material life. His bookshelves were full of philosophers like Nietzsche and Pascal, side by side with leading Swedish authors. He had developed his own individual philosophy, based equally on his own everyday experience and the fruits of his reading. I can still remember some of his questions and reflections. One in particular has stuck in my mind.

'Have you ever thought how lazy people are?' he said to me one day. 'If they can take a short-cut across the grass at the corner of a street, they nearly all will. You can be sure there'll be a trampled path over the grass, even though it would probably only take a few seconds more to go round the corner on the pavement. Yet at the same time there are people, sometimes the same people, who climb Mount Everest. Can you explain that?'

I couldn't, of course. I still can't. I'm not even sure that I want to.

Be it rain, snow or sunshine, he never fails. I know. Slowly the door opens, and he comes in as he always has: rather sad-faced, and in his eyes a distant look. He glances furtively around; it's all right, the place is empty. His heavy clogs clatter on the boards. He tries to walk quietly, but can't manage it: there is such a tremendous echo in there.

He arrives in good time for every train; at least half an hour or even an hour too early.

This is the boy who never goes on a journey!

(*Cape Farewell*)

On freedom

When Helle and I sailed into the gap between the two concrete moles of Thyborøn we were already on our way out into the North Sea in our own minds. We had listened to the Danish five-day forecast, which promised five windless days, with the one caveat that there could be winds nearing gale force 'towards the end of the period'. After a short discussion the ship's council decided unanimously to sail the next morning on the basis of the maxim 'better too little wind than too much'.

We began our preparations as soon as we had tied up. While Helle made a spicy meat stew in the pressure cooker for two dinners at sea, I bought some spare cans and carried diesel on board. When I'd finished we calculated that we would be able to motor two thirds of the way to Scotland, which ought to be enough. It was highly improbable that there wouldn't be any wind at all in the three days and nights we reckoned the crossing would take.

Later that evening, when all the preparations were completed, I sat at the chart table looking at Reed's Nautical Almanac, which contains information on every conceivable subject under the sun for the edification of seafarers. I consulted the chapter on weather and weather reports. By chance I happened upon the wavelength, frequency and time of the Norwegian maritime forecasts, which I had never listened to before: the Danish, Swedish and English were more than enough – too many cooks..., as they say. But since I was doing nothing else and it was due in ten minutes, I switched on the radio. And what did I hear? That a force eight gale warning, up to forty miles an hour, had been issued for most of the North Sea! It must be a mistake: both the Danish and the English had forecast calm conditions.

I was up at six next morning to listen to the first Danish report. The Norwegians seemed to have been right; now even the Danes had gone over to gale warnings.

The wind arrived the same day, rough and raw, from the north-west. So instead of sailing out on a calm North Sea we had to hole up for a week behind the massive breakwaters of Thyborøn with the wind whining and whistling through our rigging.

Needless to say we counted ourselves lucky that we hadn't already set sail. There was nothing inviting about a stormy North Sea. But best of all was the fact that it didn't matter when we got away. We had all the time in the world and could afford to wait. We could even give up the whole idea of sailing on if we wanted. We could stay in Thyborøn for a year or two and winter on the shores of the North Sea. We could turn round, sail south and make our way through the canals to the Mediterranean. We could even sail back to Dragør. We had enough money for at least three years' sailing and no plans that couldn't be altered according to whim, weather and wind. There was nobody waiting for us over the horizon. No one was expecting us back for a couple of years. We could do more or less whatever we wanted. We were as free as we could ever wish to be in this life.

～

But what does being free really mean? For me it is in part very simple: freedom consists of a paid-off sailing yacht and enough money to be able to live for a year or two with no plans other than ones which can be altered on the spur of the moment. Freedom is being able to wake up in *Rustica*'s cabin or somewhere else without any particular obligations to fulfil. Freedom is lying safe and sound in harbour and knowing that you can set sail at any time and go anywhere in the world. Freedom is being able to do whatever you yourself have decided you most want to do. Freedom is a diary with nothing but blank pages, a story without a full-stop.

But is that all it is?

In 1971, at the age of nineteen, I was called up for national service. It came as an unpleasant surprise: I had completely repressed the knowledge that I would have to spend a year in uniform after my school examinations.

I had scarcely set foot through the regimental gates in Karlsborg, a town on the western shore of Lake Vättern, before my previous vague feelings of reluctance and scepticism became more acute. The first shock came when we had to collect our uniforms and were ordered to put them on. I had been a loner ever since childhood, going my own way and avoiding the herd. Being a member of a gang, for instance, had never been my style.

But it was only when I got the uniform on and saw myself and the others instantly transformed from individuals into recruits, into a group of surnames with numbers, that it sank in just how deep-rooted my aversion was. The mere fact of being in uniform made me feel physically unwell. It was as if I had been put in a straitjacket, as though my very existence were threatened.

The uniform was only the start of the long process designed to mould a number of individuals into a troop, into an effective unit of the Swedish army. Not only did we have to make our beds and polish our shoes in the same way, we also had to do it together at the same time. Not only did we have to march in the same direction, we also had to do it in step. Not only did we have to look alike, we also had to be alike and behave alike.

I remember most clearly of all a sergeant teaching us how to clean our boots. He bellowed out instructions as if it were a matter of life or death and we were a bunch of bird-brained idiots. I happened to be directly in front of him and made my silent protest by consistently staring out of the window over his shoulder, but without missing a word of what he was saying. I kept having to field questions of the 'Larsson, repeat what I said!' variety, and did so every time, word for word.

But it wasn't just the army and its orders that made me feel uneasy, to put it mildly. On the Friday, before lunch, we had to collect our submachine guns. Merely holding the weapon filled me with revulsion. Yet it was obvious my reaction was not universally shared. Many of my fellow-recruits and future reserve officers emerged from the stores brandishing their guns in the air.

'We're going out to shoot!' they yelled, as if it were a game of cowboys and Indians.

All I could think of was that the weapon I had in my hand could take somebody's one and only life.

On the Monday, we were to learn to drill, march in line and about-turn on command. The exercise took place on a big gravel parade ground in bright spring sunshine. Again we had a sergeant as our instructor. He screamed out his orders, left, right, left, right, halt, quick march, in a never-ending stream. No one was surprised when, true-to-type, he called us sacks of potatoes and other less flattering epithets. He bawled out me in particular once or twice, doubtless with justification in his eyes. My whole body, backed up by my heart and to some extent by my head, fought to resist this attempt to teach us what was very pertinently called 'blind obedience'.

We must have been marching, about-turning and halting for the best part of an hour when the sergeant yelled the words that released me from my impotence: 'You're here to learn to obey without thinking!'

Alone among the group of thirty aspiring officers I stood stock still.

'Larsson, what the hell are you doing?'

'Sir,' I said, 'I request permission to speak to the major!'

I'll never understand how I had the sense to utter those particular words, but sensible it was. If I had just stood to one side or even remonstrated I would have been guilty of one of the worst crimes you can commit in the army, disobeying orders 'in front of the troops'. There is nothing the military fears more than that, because it risks undermining discipline and battle morale. In wartime it would usually be punishable by death. It is tantamount to high treason and regarded as a direct threat to the security of the state.

The sergeant granted my request without asking my reasons. He may have realised he had gone too far in his zeal, and that it would exacerbate the situation if he asked me publicly why I wanted to see the major.

I left the troop to their marching in the brilliant sunshine. As soon as I had turned my back on the sergeant and the others I knew with absolute certainty that this was my final contribution to the Swedish Army. I felt an overwhelming sense of relief and joy. The purgatory was at an end before it had really begun.

Even today I continue to be amazed at my decision. I was oblivious to the potential consequences. I hadn't taken that aspect into consideration, if 'consideration' is the right word for something that was just a mixture of thoughts and emotions that went on intensifying over the three days my call-up lasted. The decision came from within, and as soon as it was made I knew it was the only right thing for me. The whole of my being concurred. There wasn't the slightest semblance of doubt, not the slightest fear of the consequences, not the slightest inner voice sounding objections or advising care or prudence. The best description I can find to do justice to my feelings is intoxicating happiness.

The major looked faintly perplexed to see me. He had no idea why I should have requested an interview.

I explained immediately that I couldn't go on and that my decision was irrevocable. I told him what the sergeant had said. I also added that I couldn't understand how the Swedish Army could operate with officers who were permitted to bludgeon us into mindless obedience.

The major came over as quite sympathetic and fair. He made no serious attempt in this initial conversation to make me see the error of my ways, but asked me to think about it overnight. Since his request was couched in amicable terms, I agreed. But the first thing I did when I returned to barracks was to pack, hand in my uniform and machine gun and put on civilian clothes. Then I lay down on my bunk and relaxed. Great was the curiosity of my fellowrecruits when they came in. I explained my views and told them I was going home. In some eyes I saw a glimmer of yearning, in some uncomprehending astonishment or even condemnation.

Others seemed almost awe-stricken that anyone should dare to take such a step. A general feeling of delirium pervaded the group.

'You're bloody brave!' was a typical comment.

It was only when I saw their reactions, heard their questions and noticed their surreptitious glances that it dawned on me that my decision would either provoke offence or arouse admiration, that it had a moral dimension over and above saving myself from mental torment.

I went to see the major again at ten the next morning. This time he attempted to persuade me to change my mind. His tactic was to try to convince me by rational argument that Sweden had to have a strong defence. But the discussion of defence policies and war strategy was a short one. I made it clear that my problem lay elsewhere: my decision wasn't the result of rational political conviction.

When the major realised I wasn't susceptible to military arguments he offered me the option of noncombatant service. I gave an unambiguous refusal to that too. I detested violence as much then as I do now, but I am not a radical pacifist. Once again, this rejection was not a fully considered result of careful reasoning. Though sure of my convictions, I was paradoxically unaware of my innermost motivation.

I remember the major shaking my hand and wishing me good luck. He explained that the matter would now be referred to the civil courts. While waiting for my trial I would be granted home leave, as it was called. Before I left I had to go to the office – to get a train ticket warrant and draw my pay, seven kronor a day, for the three days I had served as a soldier! I told the major I would gladly donate the money to the Ministry of Defence. But right was right. I had to hurry to draw my money before lunch. I didn't want to stay any longer than was absolutely necessary.

With the exception of the end of some of the voyages already described, I have rarely been so deeply happy and contented as when I sat on the train on the way back to my home town of Jönköping. It felt as if my body and soul were a perfectly-tuned instrument. Not a jarring note, not a dissonant chord. I had made a decision that was fully in harmony with my inner being and my heartfelt convictions, whatever they were.

Three times I refused. Three times I was imprisoned, for five months in total. That was the price I had to pay to hold on to the freedom to decide for myself when, where and for what I was prepared to risk or sacrifice my life. But it took several years before I understood what really lay behind the strength of feeling that had made me a conscientious objector without considering all the ramifications. Fundamentally it was the need for freedom. Military service and above all the possibility of going into battle were just examples of duress that restricted that freedom. But being forced to risk and perhaps sacrifice your life without even giving your consent was without doubt the supreme infringement of liberty.

In court after my third and final refusal I made a speech. I explained that it was a human right, more important than any other, that every human being should be able to decide for himself when and for what he was prepared to gamble his life, and that it was a human right, the most important one of all, for young Americans to refuse to risk their lives in Vietnam, or for young Russians to do the same in Afghanistan. Military service in defence of your country was the thin end of the wedge; it was war service I had in mind.

Evidently my lecture cut no ice since I was sentenced to two more months in prison. The written verdict arrived a few weeks after the trial. I was curious to see what they had made of my speech, which had been tape-recorded. But under the heading 'court findings' there was just one line: 'Larsson doesn't want others to determine his actions!'

I won't deny that there is some truth in that laconic observation on my character. The nub of the matter was the freedom to be one's own master, from the banal level of being in a boat without fixed plans and schedules and appointments, to the deeply felt belief in asserting the right to make one's own decisions about one's own life. As far as I am concerned, time clocks are the ultimate life-denying symbols; sailing yachts the ultimate symbol for the freedom that can be experienced and lived without impacting on others.

For many people, perhaps for most, freedom is an absolute good. Few words have such a positive ring to them as 'freedom'. The reality, as always, is more complex. Some feel free by repressing others. Some are as free as it is possible to be through their wealth, but they may have earned that wealth at others' expense. The relative freedom that we have in the so-called enlightened Western democracies is to a large extent the result of the consistent exploitation and impoverishment of Third World countries.

Let us agree that freedom in pure and abstract form, if there is such a thing, is indubitably good. But the *feeling* of being free proves nothing. The subjective feeling of freedom is neither good nor evil, neither positive nor negative. There is even, though infrequently, coercion that is useful and life enhancing. Powerful and confident feelings of personal freedom are just as compatible with personal evil as with goodness, with the repression of others as with compassion for others.

So when I say that I suffer a chronic and absolute need for freedom, this should be understood literally and not necessarily as a positive quality. The problem is that it is hardly possible to live on land now, in presentday societies, without one's own freedom impinging on that of others. In our individualistic society there isn't enough solidarity, love or friendship to prevent the worst consequences of freedom and its extremes. This also applies, to a greater or lesser extent, to myself.

At sea, with a clear horizon all around, with deserted anchorages ahead, with the whole world as a potential destination and without a home port either for the boat or its crew, you can by and large live out your dream of freedom without restraint. Admittedly saving up to buy the boat, equip it and maintain yourself for a couple of years always impinges on someone. But you can live with that, at least if you have a modest-sized yacht that with a little imagination can be bought, equipped and sailed on an average salary.

∼

For sailors, sailing is a necessity, they say. But that is only half the truth. Sailing is a necessity if you want to be as free as you could wish in this life without your freedom impinging on others. If you want to be free, that is. Otherwise you're happy either way.

The world has been implacably cruel and evil, carrying a pernicious multitude through space – we can see that, but the sun above us has no morality. The world has also been very good. We can see that, but the sun above us is like a constantly swarming beehive of fire.

The sun has left us to our own devices, while faithfully casting down its solar honey through space to nourish life.

Solar honey and solar salt. We human beings are left to manage our own affairs.

(Aimless Travels)

On further adventures

This book was started on the day I first set off as skipper of my own yacht, the Folkboat *Skum*, to sail from Kalmar to Påskallavik further up the coast of the Kalmar Sound. It developed in fragmentary form during the winters we spent on board *Rustica* in Dragør. The composition took shape somewhere in Scotland and acquired flesh and blood in voyages back and forth across Celtic waters, from Cape Wrath to Finisterre.

Ten thousand nautical miles later a comma has been inserted in an eighteenth-century fisherman's house in Denmark, a stone's throw from the Kattegat, where I have anchored myself for the time being after seven years afloat. If I open the door and put my head out I can see Kullen Point on the Swedish shore opposite and the open horizon of the Kattegat to the north-west behind a conglomeration of fishing boat and yacht masts. When storms rage I can hear the thunder of the waves on the stone harbour wall and the beach. The gulls squawk here as loud as ever they did round *Rustica* in various ports during our years on board. When the wind blows from the north the smell of sea and seaweed wafts in at the windows. We hear the boom of foghorns when the mist is dense. In other words, we feel at home.

I couldn't have dreamt of anywhere better than Gilleleje when we finally decided to come ashore to create space for a new little person, our daughter Kathrine. But I still yearn. Nothing would feel less strange than once again setting up home on the sea, with no fixed abode or home port.

Now my dream is that one day Kathrine will ask me if I wouldn't like to move back on board again and spend the rest of my life sailing. It wouldn't take much to persuade me.

> That's the way it is with life and goals; it seems to end in the middle of the sea, and seems to begin in the middle of the sea, and our goal seems to be in the middle of the sea.
>
> (*Aimless Travels*)

Appendix: On voyages
(for those who are interested in routes, harbours and courses)

Many people read sailing memoirs to seek inspiration, encouragement and tips for their own dreams of casting off, whatever their degree of adventurousness. I even do so myself. Since I don't want to leave anyone disappointed, I will end by filling in some chronological details.

My first long passage was from Kalvehave on the Danish island of Sjælland to St-Malo in Brittany on the IF-boat *Moana*. Equipment was standard, with log, compass and radio direction finder our (only) navigational aids. Our means of propulsion apart from sails was an old outboard motor that sometimes failed to start at the most critical moments. For a tender we had a garish yellow inflatable of the simplest type. Some emergency flares, lifejackets and lifelines constituted our (limited) safety equipment, except for a radar reflector between the backstays. We had self-steering in the true meaning of the word: we steered ourselves the whole time. With two of us, three-hour watches – Chinese watches – were the norm. Janne Robertsson and I sailed the entire way, and Helle was with us for a third of the cruise. Our enthusiasm and caution must to some extent have compensated for the frankly inadequate equipment.

We set off through the Kiel Canal, towed by friendly people who took pity on our relative youth and unreliable motor. Our route was Borkum, Vlieland, Zeebrugge, Cherbourg, St-Malo. They were long stages, the longest being 215 nautical miles, and we seemed to be sailing mostly at night. We kept strictly to putting out with the tide astern, and that summer the tide always turned at four in the morning. More than once Janne and I woke to the confounded ringing of the alarm clock at half past three, firmly determined to set sail. But just as often we would look at one another and listen to the wind until one of us declared that it was 'probably blowing a bit too hard'. And so we would go back to sleep, which meant that we set off instead in the afternoon and thus sailed mostly at night (only later did it occur to us that it didn't actually matter if we set off in a counter-current when sailing such lengthy stages as these).

No one could pretend that the weather was ideal for relaxing sailing. *Yachting World* even published an article about that season's wind and weather: it was entitled 'A Miserable Summer'!

Typically enough we had our best weather while moored in St-Malo, warm and sunny with easterly winds for ten days.

We also did the return trip in long hops, under pressure of time rather than by choice: St-Malo – Guernsey – Cherbourg – Dunkirk – Ijmuiden – Den Helder – Holtenau – Kiel.

The whole cruise took two and a half months and covered 18,000 nautical miles.

~

The following year it was Scotland's turn, there and back in the same IF-boat, but now with a new Suzuki outboard motor, partly because we intended to sail through the Caledonian Canal. Sten Holst from Kalvehave crewed; Helle was working but flew over later to Scotland to sail with us in the Hebrides.

I took *Moana* myself the 150 nautical miles to Ålborg in the Limfjord, and Sten met me there with a borrowed life raft under his arm. I had also fitted a wind vane of the simplest type, so simple in fact that it never worked, except possibly when *Moana* was so well-trimmed that she would have sailed herself anyway. Otherwise the equipment was the same as the year before: log, compass and radio direction finder.

We took two days sailing to Thyborøn, stopping in Løgstør and Oddesund, the latter a tiny dilapidated fishing harbour that must once have seen better days. The weather was ideal, sunny with fresh easterlies.

No sooner had we tied up among Thyborøn's massive North Sea trawlers than Sten began talking about setting off immediately for Scotland, encouraged by the easy sail thus far. But I, as usual, wanted to wait and see for a day or two, and this time my innate caution was justified. We had a vicious westerly gale hammering relentlessly on the huge concrete moles of Thyborøn for the next four days. Sten and I spent a lot of time in the seamen's club, as did most of the fishermen who didn't want to venture out.

The crossing to Scotland, 340 nautical miles, took a total of eighty-nine hours, in reasonable weather and mostly favourable winds, except for the last six hours when we had a following wind of thirty-five miles an hour or so. Otherwise the best moment on that crossing was when we sighted land. The first thing I spotted was the lighthouse on Rattray Head. We had hit our target with only log and compass, despite having made thirteen changes of course because of adverse winds.

On the other hand, I had never been so tired as when we tied up in Fraserburgh. Sten had been seasick for two of our three days. He acquitted himself well and took every one of his turns at the helm, but I had to steal moments from my own three-hour watches to navigate and get myself something to eat, Sten being supremely indifferent to such culinary requirements – he ate nothing for the duration of the crossing.

After resting up for a few days we sailed into the Moray Firth, with Lossiemouth as our first port of call, before heaving to in Inverness and going through the lock into the Caledonian Canal. Then we took it easy, anchoring in the black waters of Loch Ness, mooring for a night beneath the ruins of Invergarry Castle and spending several days in Corpach before finally reaching the Atlantic.

From Corpach we sailed to Oban, the Highlands' largest town on the west coast, to which Helle came by plane and bus. Our next destination was the classic Tobermory, where all self-respecting Scotland-sailors stop over. We spent the rest of the fortnight in various anchorages in the Sound of Mull and surrounding waters, Loch na Droma Buidhe, popularly known as Drambuie, Loch Aline, Shuna Sound, Kerrera.

The return leg followed the same route, the only difference being that we set off from Buckie on the east coast of Scotland and sailed into Aalbæk, south of Skagen, after four days and five nights, long enough to get our second wind, as it were, so that we could have gone on for days without putting into port.

~

There was a gap of a few years before the next trip. We wanted to sail further and for longer, so we needed a larger boat. The only way to afford both yacht and voyage was to live on the new yacht itself, and that was *Rustica*.

After four years on board we left Langelinie marina in Copenhagen to a fanfare of trumpets and waving of hands from friends and relations. I admit to a pang in my heart as the valedictory committee faded away in both sight and sound astern. I heard later that the same feeling had been prevalent ashore. Perhaps not surprisingly when our expressed intention was to be away indefinitely, for as long as the money lasted, one year or five. Or for ever.

To begin with we sailed in *Moana*'s wake – up across the Kattegat, from Helsingør to Ålborg in a day and a night. When we put in to Ålborg it was blowing a full gale and for the next few days it gusted hurricane-force over Denmark and southern Sweden. The harbourmaster in Copenhagen actually took the trouble to get Helle's mother's telephone number to check that we hadn't been at sea when the storm broke. Boats had even torn their moorings in Langelinie and been badly damaged. But we had been lucky. We put into port only hours ahead of the worst of it. Before we sailed on I had to climb the mast and clean the lamp that was covered in a layer of Jutland's best soil – that's how ferocious the gale had been.

When the storm abated we continued through the Limfjord to Thyborøn, across the North Sea to Fraserburgh, Inverness, the Caledonian Canal and Tobermory. Only after that did we start our real voyage of discovery, though the joys of renewing acquaintance were considerable.

Oddly enough, the return to Scotland felt like coming home. From Tobermory we sailed to the Outer Hebrides, for the likes of us an unspoilt, windswept paradise of sunshine and showers. Then we spent two weeks sailing around with Helle's mother and sisters and their partners. Her mother had chartered a boat, and had arranged with Helle a surprise for me: we would be called up on the VHF radio by MacDuff, known to readers of *The Celtic Ring*. But the very day Helle knew the family would be boarding their charter boat, a strong south-easterly gale blew up and we huddled in Lochboisdale on South Uist while the rain poured down.

'There's something I'd better tell you,' Helle said with an unusual tone in her voice.

And so I heard the whole story of what all her telephone calls home had really been about. We decided it wasn't a very good idea to lure the family into unknown waters in an unfamiliar boat north of Ardnamurchan, since for Scottish sailors it was the point of no return. We headed back, and instead I was the one who rowed out in the dinghy to meet the family when they turned up in Tobermory. He who laughs last, laughs longest.

As it turned out, we could safely have let the family sail all round Scotland in those ten days. The sun shone down from clear skies, the wind was mostly conspicuous by its absence, and the island of Coll registered a record temperature of 26.9 degrees.

After ten days in various anchorages we went through the Crinan Canal together and then left the Highlands and the family behind us. We looked forward to new waters and new experiences. Even though we always felt that Ireland, Brittany and Galicia gave us good value, nowhere ever measured up to the west coast of Scotland, despite the intermittent cold, the rain that lashed down with every low pressure system, and the gale warnings that came as thick and fast as beads on a rosary.

At the other end of the Crinan Canal Sten reported for duty on *Rustica*. He was delighted with the comfort. Sailing a Rustler 31 was like driving a Rolls-Royce in comparison with the IF-boat. But he regretted not seeing the west coast again. As well he might.

We sailed with Sten to East Loch Tarbert and Campbeltown, and from there to Northern Ireland. With fences and armed guards around the marinas we never felt at ease in Ulster, despite the friendly locals. From the little fishing port of Ardglass with its snuffling giant seals we sailed direct to Howth and Dublin, where both Sten and Helle signed off. Helle had to go home and work for two months. After a week and a half in port waiting for a new inflatable dinghy as a replacement for the Optimist dinghy *Sussi*, which despite our tackle was much too heavy and unsteady, I began my solo trip to Cork, two hundred nautical miles via Wicklow, Arklow and Dunmore East. I stopped in Crosshaven, which is where Janne Robertsson came to sail the south-west coast with me and take a look at Fastnet Rock. We spent a week doing that, and found the ideal harbour to overwinter: Kinsale, just south of Cork.

My winter in Kinsale with Helle will remain the memory of a lifetime, among many others on that trip. But it would need a book of its own.

Before we left Ireland, having survived the winter, Helle and I attempted to sail the south-west coast again. We put out on the first of April in fantastic spring weather, of which we then saw no further sign for the ensuing month. But we had interesting experiences anyway, as the only leisure craft cruising so early in the season. We managed to reach Crookhaven, a magnificent anchorage as far south-west as you can go, before we turned back to Kinsale to gather our strength, exhausted by the gales and constant howling in the rigging.

A fortnight later we left Ireland for good, with a great sense of loss. The two hundred nautical miles across the Irish Sea to Newlyn took us a day and a half, with some difficulty because of engine failure after only three hours at sea. We got the diagnosis in Falmouth: a broken cylinder head that cost us £800 to replace.

After another fortnight we chugged away from Britain on half power – we couldn't do more while we were running in the new head – and sailed over to Tréguier in Brittany. By that point we knew that our days of complete freedom were numbered. I had heard that I could have my old job back as research assistant at the university, the same post that had so appositely been terminated through lack of funds at the very moment we had gathered together enough funds ourselves to go off on our travels. With some mental anguish I accepted. It would be hard to imagine a job with more freedom than research assistant. You have a modest amount of teaching, no obligation to be present otherwise and 'only' have to produce one piece of research of a certain standard. (Which I hasten to add, in case of prejudiced views to the contrary, does not mean that you don't have to work; the truth is rather the opposite – university research assistants are very cost-effective for the state: on average they work far longer than forty hours a week, without getting a penny in overtime. Anyone who doesn't believe it need only ask the university night security guards.)

From now on we would have to be at home in the winter and sail in summer, even though the latter could be three whole months if we were lucky. Having sailed the north coast of Brittany that summer, we decided to leave the yacht right there in Tréguier, a town we had fallen for, with a protected yacht marina far inland.

Since I was research assistant in French this plan also had the advantage that I could travel down in winter, check the boat and do some work at the same time, which among other things meant simply keeping up my linguistic proficiency. I did so for three weeks in January.

On 20th May of that year we set off again and sailed round Brittany at a leisurely pace until we came to Belle Ile. There we made ready to cross the Bay of Biscay. The 240 nautical miles to Gijón in Asturias took two and a half days, after which we sailed the waters of the north and north-west corner of the Spanish coast. In Galicia we sailed in and out of almost every *ría*, each in turn seeming increasingly magnificent, but nevertheless without the same friendly atmosphere ashore as in Ireland.

Then once again it was time to leave *Rustica* to her own devices, always painful, and return to the greyness of everyday life, which means for me days whose content is known in advance. This time we decided on Vila-garcía at the head of the Ría de Arousa, not because of the town itself, which is as ugly as sin, but because of the marina and transport links.

Yet it turned out that the marina was nowhere near as sheltered as it

172

appeared to be. I flew over for two weeks in January to attend to *Rustica*, and when I got there the wind was so strong that my plane was the last one allowed to land, very bumpily, at Santiago de Compostela airport. And the gales continued unabated for two weeks. Even the locals, who were used to winter storms, had seldom seen the like. Galicia had such heavy rainfall that large areas of the region were flooded. So much fresh water ran out into the *rías* that the mussels in the big mussel-beds died. Scarcely a day went by without news of a vessel in difficulties. It was almost impossible to live on *Rustica*, even for me who had lived on board for five years. She rolled and pitched so violently in harbour that you couldn't stand a coffee cup on the table, and so much on one unlucky occasion that the top of her mast hit the mast of the neighbouring yacht. The masthead lamp and radio aerial were smashed to pieces. I stayed in a hotel for three nights just to get some sleep. And another night I went to the same hotel because I couldn't even get aboard from the narrow heaving pontoon alongside.

Some may wonder how we 'dared' leave *Rustica* in such a distant and unprotected place at all. Weren't we afraid of theft, for instance? As far as the latter was concerned, the risk was far less than back home, because there were harbourmasters on duty twentyfour hours a day. And I had rarely seen a harbour that appeared so well protected from wind and weather. There was just one thing I had overlooked: the long concrete jetty of the industrial port which ran at right angles to the opening to the yacht marina. The waves in the *ría* were never higher than two metres, even in hurricane-force winds, and the Atlantic swell never came in that far. But the waves bounced off the concrete jetty and surged straight into the marina, where they struck *Rustica* abeam.

After another winter, this time at home, we decided to sail to Ireland. Our intention was to leave the yacht in Scotland in the future, since this after all was where we preferred to sail. We set out from Vilagarcía to Camariñas, north of Cape Finisterre, the ideal starting point for crossing the Atlantic to Ireland. We lay up there for a week while deep depressions with violent winds passed over to the north. It gave Helle the opportunity to check her suspicions. A testing kit purchased at the local chemist's dispelled any doubt: she was pregnant.

At a stroke, a lot, if not everything, was changed. We are not hard men of the sea, as I have already intimated. Rather the opposite. Having spent a further week listening to the gale warnings for the Irish Sea we decided to have *Rustica* sailed home by professionals: they wouldn't run the risk of pregnancy sickness. So we rang a delivery firm in England and a few days later two men arrived on the quayside in Camariñas to take over *Rustica* and sail her all the way home in a fortnight for about £1,500 (six dollars per nautical mile), roughly the same as it would have cost us to have the boat moored in Scotland and to fly over to sail and maintain her.

We took delivery of *Rustica* in Brunsbüttel at the entrance to the Kiel Canal and went sailing round Denmark, especially the islands south of Fyn, for three weeks of sunshine and light winds. It was a mixed experience. It was a relief not to have to put up with the eternal swell and relentless tides that had been such a part of our life since we left Denmark. It was fantastic in its way to have so many harbours and anchorages always within reach. But it was a shock to find just how *many* boats were sailing our waters and crowding into our harbours. In a well-frequented anchorage in Galicia, Scotland or Ireland there would be a handful of boats at most. In Denmark you could always more than quadruple the numbers. It can be difficult to find a reasonable place in a harbour if you arrive too late in the afternoon. And above all – no one is interested in who you are or where you've come from. No one feels any need to invite you in for a drink and a chat in a cosy cabin. We don't either. Sailing in the Baltic so easily becomes anonymity and consumption, no more and no less, the very opposite of what we sail for.

Rustica is now safe and sound in Gilleleje harbour. I hope she is happy, with a fixed home port for the first time in our ownership. But at the same time I am almost sure that she, like me, feels there is something missing. Spending your days dreaming of what is lurking over the horizon is all very well, but it is not the same as setting off in a beautiful and seaworthy sailing yacht to explore for oneself.

~

Postscript: After much agonising *Rustica* was sold in the summer of 1999 and is now sailing the waters of the Swedish west coast. She is in good hands. In my boat-free year I suffered severe withdrawal symptoms. Paradoxically enough I feel insecure without a boat. For me, a boat has always been the ultimate safety valve. My suffering was short-lived, however. There is now a new yacht in Gilleleje, a *Bulle de Soleil*, designed by the French naval architect Caroff, who specialises in long-distance boats. It is a stronglybuilt steel 38-footer, not as pretty as *Rustica*, but with character and other qualities, particularly a centreboard, which provides new and undreamt-of possibilities. With the centreboard up she draws only just over two feet and can dry out at low tide! There won't be a bay where we can't anchor, not a harbour we can't put into. We have named the new yacht *Stornoway*. We'll be sailing her there in two years' time.